Let the Bums Burn

Australia's deadliest building fire
and the Salvation Army tragedies

Other Books By Geoff Plunkett

Chemical Warfare in Australia

Death by Mustard Gas

Let the Bums Burn

Geoff Plunkett

Published by LEECH CUP BOOKS
Berowra Heights, Sydney, Australia

http://www.deadliestfire.info

Printed by Lightning Source
Edited by Cathy Johnstone
Design and Typsetting by Geoff Plunkett

Set in Minion Pro (text) & Adobe Garamond Pro (titles)

National Library of Australia Cataloguing-in-Publication entry

Author: Plunkett, Geoff, author.

Title: Let the bums burn : australia's deadliest building fire and the salvation army tragedies / Geoff Plunkett.

ISBN: 9780987427939 (paperback).

Notes: Includes index.

Subjects: 1. Salvation Army--Australia--History.
2. Disasters--Australia--History.
3. Accidents--Australia--History.
4. Public buildings--Fires and fire prevention--Australia.
5. Fires--Casualties--Australia--Statistics.
6. Fires--Australia--History.
7. Fires--Australia--Case studies.
8. Fires--Australia--Statistics.
9. Fires--Safety measures.
10. Fire investigation--Australia.
11. Fire prevention--Australia.
12. Fire sprinklers--Australia.

Dewey: 363.340994

Dedication

To All Those Involved

The William Booth Memorial Home After The Fire
Coroner's Report

The People's Palace, Adelaide
Salvation Army

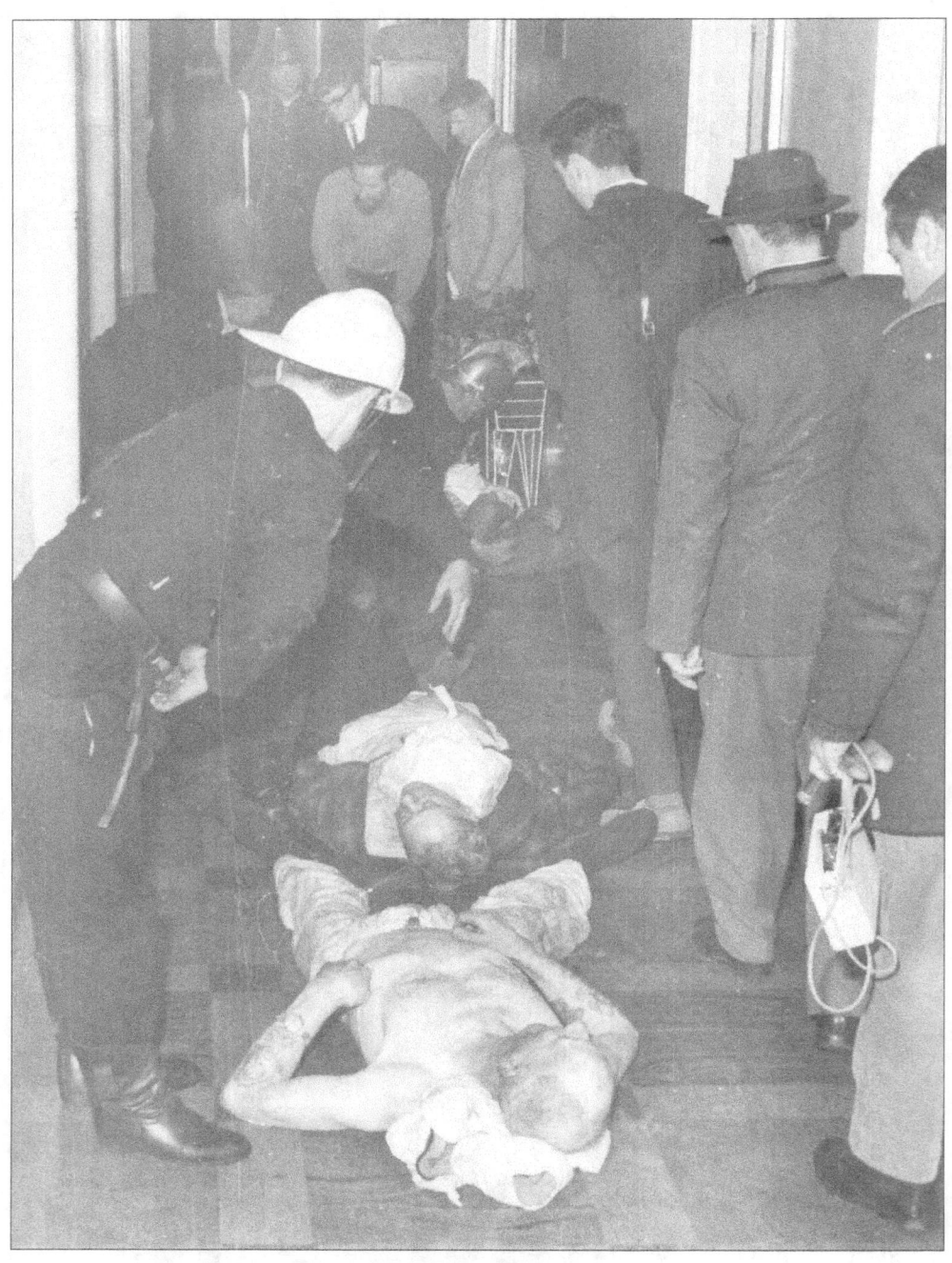

Casualties in the Central Hallway of the William Booth Memorial Home. Two Police 'Roundsmen', Reporters based in the Press-Room next to the Russell Street Police Headquarters, are visible in the rear. Ken Hickey (Glasses) and Noel Harley (Notepad).
Salvation Army

Table of Contents

Quotes x
Poem xii
Roll Call. xiv
Introduction xvi
Chapter 1 – The William Booth Memorial Home. 1
Chapter 2 – The People's Palace 51
Chapter 3 – The Case for Sprinklers. 65
Appendix 1 – Australian Building Fires Since 1966. . 73
Appendix 2 – Deadliest US Fires By Decade 74
References 75
Acknowledgements 76
Endnotes 79
List of Photographs and Maps 85
Index 88

Quotes

They drift in from time to time — some might stay for a day, some for a week and others for a year. Some of them drink heavily and we hope we are a good, steadying influence on them. Many people cannot understand why we bother with these types. We act in mercy, not judgement.

Colonel R. Darlow, Social Secretary, Salvation Army, 14 August 1966 (one day after the fire)
The Age, 15 August 1966

One of the matters which must have a bearing on any comment I may make about the building at 462 Little Lonsdale Street, Melbourne, is the pressing need for more of this type of shelter. Although private enterprise and government enterprise caters fairly well for the family man, and is continuing to cater for his needs, only charitable and/or religious organisations, assisted to a limited degree by public funds, make provision for the man living by himself who is handicapped by aberrations and who is in need of shelter.

H.W. Pascoe, City Coroner, 21 December 1966

Some people criticise the men who are down, but do not lift them; others preach at them, but do not lift them. Others stand on a platform, and tell them to come up, but the Salvation Army has done a good deal in going down to lift them — doing something while they are in their downward condition that harmonies with their need, with a view to bringing them up. We hope these men are going to be brought up. These institutions have been signally successful in getting men lifted.

The Salvation Army Commissioner, William Booth Memorial Home opening speech, 26 January 1916.
The War Cry, 5 February 1916

RED SHIELD

Salvation Army Red Shield
Salvation Army

LET THE BUMS BURN

Poem

Opened 26 January 1916 — Closed 16 December 1967

**IN MEMORY OF THE WILLIAM BOOTH HOSTEL
THE DAY A HOSTEL DIED**

*It was Saturday December Sixteen the year was 67,
The men have gone to homes elsewhere, for notice had been given,
The scene was sad and silent as we tacked upon the door,
A notice; which read like this — Accommodation here; is no more.*

*To many men this was their Home from five to fifty years,
I spoke to some of these poor chaps whose eyes were filled with tears
They told me it was hard to part with Home and its surrounds,
To go to somewhere strange to them; with unfamiliar sounds.*

*This Hostel when t'was opened as a Memorial to William Booth,
Was there to house the needy men, some good, some rough, uncouth,
Yet all who came beneath its doors or slept beneath its roof,
Were reminded by word or precept that the Ways of God are Truth,
For Truth and Righteousness of Life Exalteth Men on High,
And all who enter Heaven must follow this way, ere they die.*

*So the Hostel doors are now fast closed and the cubicles are bare,
The lift is almost silent; and the ever winding stair,
These same which carried traffic to the rooms upon each floor,
Have memories which awaken us to men we see no more.*

POEM

We say farewell, this Hostel, with its name of William Booth,
Where some men learned to love the Lord and follow life and truth,
To men who would exploit us, and try to "take us in"
We pray that God will save them, and take away their sin,
So may God Bless and Prosper every effort of the past,
And help us to be Faithful as we face another task.

    Stephen Henry Berry (Brigadier)
    Manager of William Booth Hostel
    Written after the building closure

Found in Salvation Army records

LET THE BUMS BURN

Roll Call

William Booth Memorial Home 1966

Leonard Hugh Baguley (aka Leonard Sault), Boot Finisher, 41

William Arthur Biske (aka William Arthur Marchant), 55

Farnsworth J Black (aka Jimmy Black), Council Cleaner, 55

James Blackwood, Cleaner Melbourne Harbour Trust, 54

Francis James Conway, Baker, 69

David Albert Cooper, Part-time Gardener, 75

Harry Dawson, Retired, 70

James Dean (aka Jim Reid), Cook and Cleaner, 53

James Edward Farr, Pensioner, 62

Vincent Gregory Fox, Chemist, 61

Frederick Johann Haas (John Frederick Haas?), Cleaner, 74

David George Hartley, Sweeper, 45

Edward William Mealor Hooson, Labourer, 61

Edward Lamaur (Lamour?), Pensioner, 65

John Russell Lloyd, Commissionaire, 49

Ronald Ernest Mackenzie, Slaughterman, 46

Joseph Dunleigh Mangan, Leading Hand Ganger, 63

John Alexander McKenzie, Boiler Attendant, 57

Herbert Joseph McNeice, Harrier then Pensioner, 84

ROLL CALL

James Robert Miller, Boilermaker, 74

Garnet Ridley Maurice Quinlan, Electricity Commission, 49

George Robertson, Gardener, 71

Andrew Showler, Labourer, 65

Charles Henry Statton, Painter, 61

Frank Udale, Labourer, Retired Pensioner, 65

James Henry Vickerman, Labourer, 55

Arthur James Vigor, Hotel Cleaner, 72

Gordon Station Whelan (Stanley Gordon Whelan?), Invalid Pensioner, 60

Thomas Raymond Wilson (aka Thomas Douglas Densworth, Raymond Densworth), Labourer, 48

James Kenneth Wright, Storeman, 65

The People's Palace 1975

Robert Murray Belton, 30

Keith Noel Burns

Douglas John Fort, 30

Steven Christopher Jones, Railway Clerk, 18

David Lindsay Roberts, Concrete Paving, 32

William Frank Simm, Taxi Driver, 30

James Andrew Turner

Introduction

Opium dens, prostitution, slums, crime, poverty and larrikinism[1]— this neighbourhood was in desperate need for the hand of God. Spiritual enlightenment came to the Little Lon district of Melbourne in 1916 in the form a Salvation Army home for destitute men: society's rejects, those pitied but ignored, those described at their funeral as 'nobodies'.[2]

Was this an attempt to proselytize, to bring God's word to a heathen cesspit, a notorious slum and red light precinct? There is a simpler reason — the soldiers of God simply cared. It was — and is — in the Salvation Army's (colloquially known as the Salvos) DNA to give practical social service and this group of men needed a home, if only for a day.

The home was located with the residents in mind; handy to the train station, close to the docks and not too far from the markets. Originally,

William Booth
Salvation Army

INTRODUCTION

the Salvation Army's Workman's Metropole in King Street had been the refuge used by 'homeless troubled working men', but when this became the Army's People's Palace in 1904, the men could not afford it.[3]

The site for the new residence, 462 Little Lonsdale Street, was purchased in 1913 and opened on Foundation Day, 26 January 1916 (now Australia Day). The Salvation Army Commissioner's speech at the opening ceremony was interrupted by a shout of 'three cheers for the Governor', the culprit being a dame who 'had made the acquaintance of King Alcohol'. In good cheer, salvationists and civilians alike took up the chant. Spurred by the lady in question, the Victorian Governor addressed the audience on the problem of drink and opined that housing the men 'would keep them from the public-house.'[4]

The men's new castle, both figuratively and literally (the building had fake battlements) provided private rooms in the heart of Melbourne's central business district for three to five shillings per week. Meals were 'astonishingly cheap', a penny for soup and bread, butter or cakes and scones; threepence for a meal including meat and vegetables. Fifty years later, the cost of a room was still less than a dollar a day.[5]

The building was erected as a memorial to William Booth, the founder and first General of the Salvation Army, who had been 'promoted to glory' only four years previously.[6] It was thus named the William Booth Memorial Home but to the residents it was simply the William Booth. This home added one more to the Army's 1200 social institutions then ministering to the poor and needy. War privation led to a delay in the first shipment of blankets, so the full complement of beds was not available for the first two weeks. However, in a short time all the rooms were occupied and the demand never eased. The residents thanked God for the Salvos.

Just past the entry foyer, there was a combined reading and smoking room with books on travel, history, religion and more. It also housed an organ for the musically talented. Singing was encouraged, cards and gambling were not. Boarders could meet visitors in a private reception room. Many moving scenes had occurred here: men had reconciled with their wives or acknowledged past wrongs.[7] Some had even found God but this was not pushed, religious interest was an elective. The Salvos understood worldly issues were more pressing; shelter and food came first.

A few of the men worked but most were pensioners, some invalids. The penniless were not forgotten either. In the early decades up to 200 meals and 30 beds were made available for free.[8] Some stayed a day, others for more than fifty years. All were troubled.

Western Wall of the William Booth Post Fire
Coroner's Report

INTRODUCTION

Fifty years of continuous service was shattered on 13 August 1966 when a catastrophic fire devastated two floors and killed 30 of its residents. The William Booth never fully recovered and closed its doors to lodgers on 16 December 1967.

At the time of the great fire half of the lodgers were 'heavy' drinkers and another quarter drank. Two-thirds of those who died had alcohol in their systems, up to a death-defying blood alcohol level of 0.433.[9] The residents reflected the general populace in that alcoholism was a symptom of greater problems, not the cause itself. Alcoholism arises from a complex combination of genetic, psychological, and environmental factors and can visit anyone through injury, organic means or dint of circumstance.

There were those estranged from their families. One fire victim, James Farr, was typical. His family broke up when he was small boy and for fifty years he had no contact with his kin. Half the men who perished were never claimed by a relative. There was mental illness but there was also much talent. A former resident was a circus sword swallower who had travelled the world plying his trade. He hung his blade above his bed to remember the glory days. Another was a dishevelled old man with a long matted beard who shuffled around the Melbourne streets carrying a couple of billycans and a bible. At night he would be found stooped next to his candle (he shunned electric light) reading his Latin and Greek books, surrounded by his bible collection. Educated at an English university, drink had got the better of him.[10]

A staggering variety of personalities passed through its doors, from the World War I diggers down on their luck to the tragic victims of the depression years, the unemployed men (mainly young) who would doss down for the night, after another fruitless day looking for work.[11]

Ask any Australian which building fire was Australia's deadliest and they may mention the Whiskey Au Go Go Nightclub or one of the several backpackers' fires but none will have heard of the 30 deaths in the William Booth in 1966. A search of Google reveals little and it would appear that the reason is that the death of a group of alcoholic rejects is neither noteworthy nor memorable.[12] Few cared when they were alive, less so when they were dead. The fire made the headlines briefly but quickly faded from consciousness to the point where the only ones who remember are the firefighters who attended the tragedy. They do not forget the makeshift morgue in the ground floor dining room, the terrified, mainly elderly men wandering like zombies throughout the building. They remember the death stares; eyes and mouths open, faces blackened by soot. They cannot forget.

Tragedy was to strike a Salvation men's residence a second time, in 1975. An area of the People's Palace in Pirie Street, Adelaide, was reserved for working men who sought affordable accommodation. As alcohol was also an issue with this cohort, they were segregated in an isolated area above the Adelaide Congress Hall, in the south side of the building. The north side of the Palace had bedrooms popular with Salvationist families attending the annual congress, or embarking on a vacation.

A fire in the early hours of 22 April 1975 incinerated seven of the boarders in the 'Tipperary' section. But while the fire at the William Booth was an accident, the origin of the fire in the Tipperary section

Tipperary Rear Escape Stairs, The People's Palace
Coroner's Report

INTRODUCTION

of the People's Palace was tainted with a strong suspicion that it was deliberately torched, a case of murder by arson.

Once both fires started, the ensuing chain of events was all too familiar to fire historians. The fires ignited combustible materials within the building, which in turn ignited the flammable wooden structure. There were locked exits, insufficient or no fire doors, no alarms and untrained staff. Most crucially, a simple lifesaving device, invented in 1874, was absent: water sprinklers.

None of these considerations, however, were on anyone's mind at the William Booth when a resident decided that it would be a good idea to start a fire in his room at the home in the afternoon of 20 December 1965.

Faulty Fireproof Door on the William Booth 3rd Floor
Coroner's Report

Salvation Army Crest and its Reference to the 'Fire' of the Holy Spirit
Salvation Army

The William Booth Memorial Home

Melbourne

20 December 1965

1.30 pm. John Buckle, a boarder at the William Booth, was furious. He was going to teach them a lesson. He smashed the radio, then the alarm clock. The remnants were strewn across his second floor room.

He was not going to let the men of the William Booth make fun of him anymore and he knew how to get their attention. A fire was a suitable punishment — that would make them think twice, for sure.

Buckle fetched a newspaper and ripped it to pieces, carefully placing the shreds on the floor next to his bed. Next, he pulled the bed sheets and blankets off the bed and placed these onto the pile. With sufficient fuel, he lit the paper and stood back.

The paper caught fire quickly, the blanket more slowly. However, within 30 seconds, the fire was established and his work was done. Buckle left the room but stayed on the second floor just to make sure someone noticed. Once the fire was discovered, Buckle left the building.

The fire grew to include the adjacent flooring, mattress and wardrobe to which it caused extensive damage but early detection enabled the fire to be extinguished quickly. The only damage was to Buckle's rented cubicle and reputation; he would spend six months in jail.[13]

This was not the first fire at the William Booth. There had been at least ten earlier fires: several in the men's private rooms, one in the kitchen, another in a lift and ironically one next to a fire hydrant.[14] There had never been any casualties and there was no reason to expect one, the building met all the fire codes.

Fatefully however, with this latest fire, the staff of the men's home had learned a questionable lesson. They believed they were able to control a fire without contacting the fire brigade.

13 August 1966

Some say it was a typical Melbourne August day, cold and wet. For Kelvin Fitness, the nightwatchman at the William Booth Memorial Home, the expectation was for a typical working day. Officially starting at 9.30 pm, his role was to survey the building every hour to make sure everything was in order. During his time there, the nights had been remarkably free of incident but this night was to become a night to remember.

Brought up in a Salvo family (with his father a Brigadier) it was almost inevitable he would land such a role. He had come from New Zealand to Melbourne for a short visit, which had now stretched to a year. Fitness enjoyed the work and as a bonus, he had somewhere to stay. He slept on the third floor, on the opposite side to where the trouble would begin. Fitness loved playing the cornet with the South Melbourne

Kelvin Fitness and Wife
Kelvin Fitness

Army Corps and was not a bad singer either, sometimes accompanying one of the residents on the ground floor piano.

Also present was Major Reiger, the Assistant Manager of the William Booth. Very likeable, he and his wife went out of their way to help the appreciative nightwatchman. Major Reiger was strict, an essential attribute in dealing with the alcoholism but he was fair and had a good rapport with both clients and staff. Things had to be right: follow his rules and you were given a chance, play up and you were out.[15] One of the residents he had a close eye on was a brandy drinker on the third floor, Vincent Gregory Fox.

Vincent Fox was born in 1903 in Hobart. A qualified pharmacist he enlisted for military service in 1942. He was initially attached to the 111 Australian General Hospital (AGH) in Tasmania and then the 107 AGH in Darwin. He is believed to have still been working as a chemist at the time of the fire. In March 1942, Fox was given a severe reprimand with 'conduct prejudice of good order' but further details of his behaviour are not specified.[16] Of average height, 5 feet 6 inches, he had ginger hair and prominent gold teeth. He was severely overweight in 1966, carrying 14 stone and had significant heart disease.

Fox was a creature of habit, a drinking habit. At 5.00 pm on most days, but always on this day, a Saturday, he opened his cubicle door on the third floor to make his brandy pilgrimage from the William Booth, his residence of the last few years.

As Fox stepped out of the room, he could almost touch the floor's firefighting equipment. A few feet to his right and abutting his room was a recess housing both a 2.5 inch canvas fire hose and an extinguisher. They looked modern and well-maintained and in fact, they were checked every six months by the Melbourne Fire Brigade.

The hose was connected to a 'wet riser' — a pipe filled with water from the street water main. It was capable of delivering a powerful torrent of 48 pounds[17] of pressure in an instant, with a simple turn of the tap, enough to quell an incipient fire.

Next to the fire hydrant (known as a millcock) was the fire escape. Adjacent to Fox's room was the southern stairwell, which led directly to the ground floor three flights below. The hydrants were located next to

Wet Riser in the Fire Fighting Recess Next to Fox's Room
Coroner's Report

the front and rear staircases for a good reason — to be within easy reach of the fire brigade. There was another advantage with this arrangement, if a floor was inaccessible due to fire, the brigade could run a hose from the level below.

In the event of a blaze Fox would be in the safest location in the building, he had direct access to both the fire escape and firefighting equipment. This was important, as 64 private rooms were jammed into the third floor, a pattern replicated on the first, second and fourth stories.[18] The rooms, although private, were tiny, measuring 7 feet 6 inches square, enough to fit a bed and few clothes but little else. The cubicles were grouped into lots of six on both sides of a north to south passage. They were accessed by narrow dead end passages running west to east. They were in fact rooms within a room. The cubicles were temporary structures within the cavernous space of each floor. With

THE WILLIAM BOOTH MEMORIAL HOME

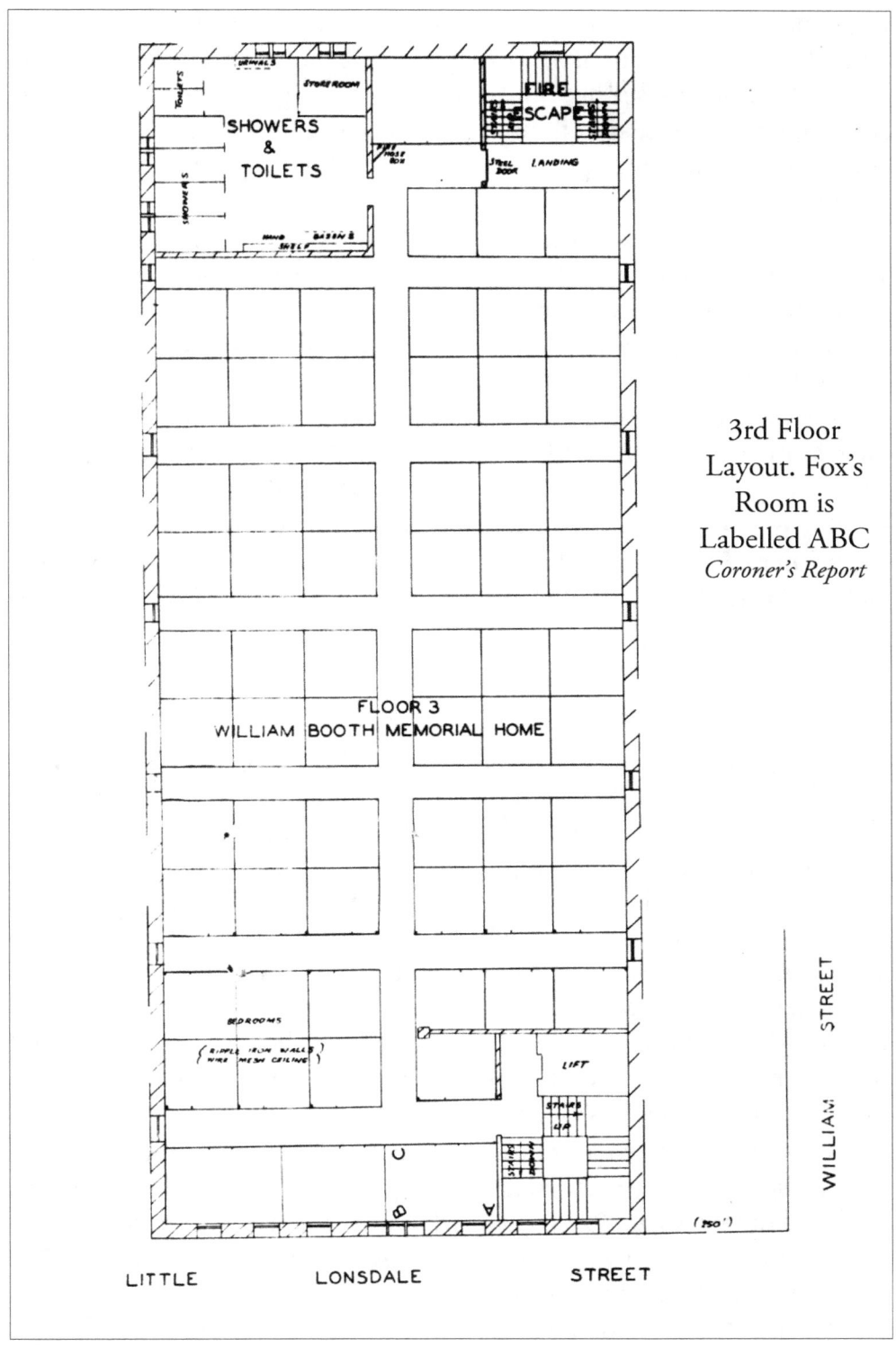

3rd Floor Layout. Fox's Room is Labelled ABC
Coroner's Report

a height of 7 feet 6 inches, there was an 11 foot gap between the top of each cubicle and the floor ceiling. A rabbit warren would be a valid description of this set-up, but under the lodging standards of the day it was completely legal and more than the government could offer. The men did not complain, they were grateful to have a space they could call home.

Fox paid no attention to the fire suppression equipment; his focus was on his next drink and the lift across the passage from the fire equipment. Fox entered the lift exiting on the bottom floor and then the home, passing under a large portrait of William Booth and into the frigid street.

Fox was not one for conversation but would say hello to the residents. He was unremarkable in this regard. Many residents kept to themselves, there were troubled pasts that they preferred to forget.

Fox made his way to his watering hole, the Metropolitan Hotel on the corner of William and Little Lonsdale Streets, only a few minutes' walk away. It was the Booth residents' pub of choice and for many their second home.

David Ferguson, an employee of the British Phosphate Commission, had also lived at the Salvos home for several years and lived directly above Fox on the fourth floor.[19] He had returned to the William Booth from a football game at 2.00 pm and slept in the afternoon. When he awoke, he also made his way to the Metropolitan Hotel for a beer. He spotted Fox soon after he arrived at 6.00 pm, by which time Fox had been drinking for just over an hour. Ferguson noted Fox was his usual self, reserved and with no slur in his voice. Ferguson knew most nights Fox was 'full' but as an established alcoholic, he held his drink well and there was no swagger. After a cursory conversation, Ferguson went out for the night leaving Fox to contemplate his next brandy.

Fox left the Metropolitan at 6.45 pm, having been there for just under two hours, and returned to the William Booth. He had a blood alcohol content of 0.392, a level which in the average person could lead to unconsciousness, a coma and possibly death. A level of 0.35 is considered the level of surgical anaesthesia. However, as Fox always had alcohol in his system, this was merely a top-up. It was estimated he had consumed three 6 ounce glasses (over 18 ounces of brandy or more than half a litre) during his short stint at the pub.[20]

As Fox re-entered the main foyer he passed a sign on the outside of the booking office cubicle. Installed three months earlier, it read:

PLEASE
OBSERVE
RADIATORS
ARE
NOT
ALLOWED
TO BE USED
IN BEDROOMS
FIRE AND ELECTRICITY PRECAUTION
WILL NOT PERMIT

Fox paid no attention to the sign even though Major Reiger had strategically placed it so 'nobody could miss it.'[21] Three months earlier, Reiger's attention had been drawn to the risk by a blown fuse, unable to cope with a surge in the current. On investigation, the Major had found a drunk resident in bed with an active double-bar radiator in his room. Realising the combination of alcohol and an exposed bar heater could be lethal, Reiger confiscated the radiator and gave the man his marching orders. He was booked out the next morning.

To reinforce the decree Reiger had also placed a warning on every receipt. Every boarder making a payment received the notice:

The use of spirit stoves and electrical appliances prohibited

Booking Clerk Ernest Reid in his Cubicle
Coroner's Report

Major Reiger had spoken directly to Fox about having a radiator in his third floor room so Fox knew he could be evicted. Fatefully he was not and why he was spared while the other man was expelled is unknown. Although there was a room cleaner on each floor who regularly accessed the rooms and was obliged to report misdemeanours, they were not allowed to examine personal items so radiators and other banned items could be hidden in bags. It was not feasible to search everyone using the lift or stairwells.

Fox returned to his cubicle in room 1 around 6.50 pm. Shivering in the winter cold, he retrieved his heater from its place of concealment. It was a 1000-watt radiant rod heater with protective wires over the front.

The Heater that Caused the Fire and a Table showing the Effects of a Backdraft and Flashover
Coroner's Report

He plugged it into the socket above his bed. Reiger had every reason to be concerned about Fox — the fate of 30 men was sealed. Like their benefactor, they would be promoted to glory within three hours.

The tragedy started when Fox knocked over the heater. Like rays from the sun, the heat from the upturned appliance radiated onto the linoleum raising its temperature. It slowly melted and vaporised, releasing a myriad of toxic gases in the process. Once the linoleum was gone, the surface layer of the wooden floor was exposed. Wood does not burn — this is an extraordinary and little understood fact. As the wooden floor was heated, a process called pyrolysis (decomposition) was initiated. The heat began to break down the surface layer forming a blackened char. In addition, flammable gases were released and it was these that ignited, forming the flame we recognise as fire. The flame inched slowly across the floor, reaching the electrical cord attached to the heater. It burnt through, exposing the wires, which touched each other.

Charred Area of the Floor where the Upturned Heater Burnt
Coroner's Report

James Cannard, the third floor cleaner, had also been at the footy match.[22] When he returned to the William Booth, he glanced at the wall clock as he entered the building: precisely 8.35 pm. As he lived in the room next to Fox's he took the lift to the third floor, noticing nothing untoward as he passed Fox's room. Cannard unlocked his door and entered, taking off his overcoat and switching on the lights. There was no response as he flicked the switch so he tried again. The same — the light was dead.

Concluding that the lights were fused Cannard left the room and returned to the bottom floor by the lift. He approached the affable booking clerk Ernest Reid (who had been in this role for 25 years) and told him he believed the lights were blown.[23] Reid responded he would have a look and knowing the fuse box was up the wall went for the ladder. With the ladder retrieved, they went up in the lift together, passing room 1 where again there was no sign of anything amiss. No flame, no smoke, no noise.

In fact, room 1 was very much alive and had been for around two hours. The flame had spread laterally as more of the floor was exposed and a blackened cavity formed directly under the heater. A plume of hot gases arose from the incipient flames. The plume included deadly carbon monoxide and other toxic materials. Being hotter than the surrounding air, the gases rose to the Masonite ceiling and fanned across to the walls. The temperature at the top of the room was now much hotter than the bottom half and as more of the room burned, this super-heated layer, rich with fuel, grew larger and banked down towards the floor. The heat cracked the windows but they stayed intact.

When Cannard and Reid arrived in the third floor corridor, the lighting was poor, possibly due to the hall light being out. Cannard retrieved his torch from his room and went along the south-north passage and into a side passage next to room 39. Here the fuse box was located on the west wall. There were three sets of six cubicles between the fuse box and Fox's room.

Reid used Cannard's torch to look over the box. There was a fuse (called a wedge) noticeably different from the others which were generally dirty and dusty. Reid looked up, 'This must be the fuse. Have a look at that.' Although it was new compared to the rest, one end had a black mark. Cannard concurred that this was the culprit.

Reid said he would go for a replacement downstairs. He always had a couple of spares prepared with new fuse wire. Cannard went with Reid to the end of the main corridor, next to the lift and awaited Reid's return opposite room 1. On Reid's return, he inserted the replacement fuse in the main hall fuse box but there was a flash as the new fuse blew again. The circuit was still overloaded so Reid returned to the bottom floor, none the wiser as to the cause.

Inside Fox's cubicle, the conditions were developing into an extraordinary fire event. This was possible because Fox's room (and the other two on the southern wall) had one crucial difference from the others on the floor. It had a hardboard (Masonite) ceiling and was closed in. The other rooms were open-top cubicles, covered in cyclone mesh, placed to prevent the men entering each other's rooms. All the cubicles had linoleum floors and walls made of two sheets of corrugated iron.

Despite the Hollywood blockbuster of the same name,[24] a backdraft (or flashback) is a rare phenomenon, which requires a special set of circumstances. The life of a fire in an enclosed space is a special beast. Because the fire in the sealed cubicle had been burning for a considerable time the lifeblood of the fire had been consumed and the oxygen level in the room had decreased to the point where the fire was suffocating. Although the flames had been strangled, the upper part

Fuse Box Next to Room 39
Coroner's Report

The Construction of Fox's Room Enclosed with a Masonite Ceiling
Coroner's Report

of the room was still superheated with an explosive mix of flammable gases, awaiting the reintroduction of the missing elixir.

~

Just after 8.40 pm, Major Reiger strode purposely into the William Booth for his nightly inspection. He entered the back way as his residence was at the rear of the home. Reiger first examined the dining room and passed on to the smoke room. Things were going smoothly. He then came around to the front office where Reid informed him of the fuse that had blown on the third floor.

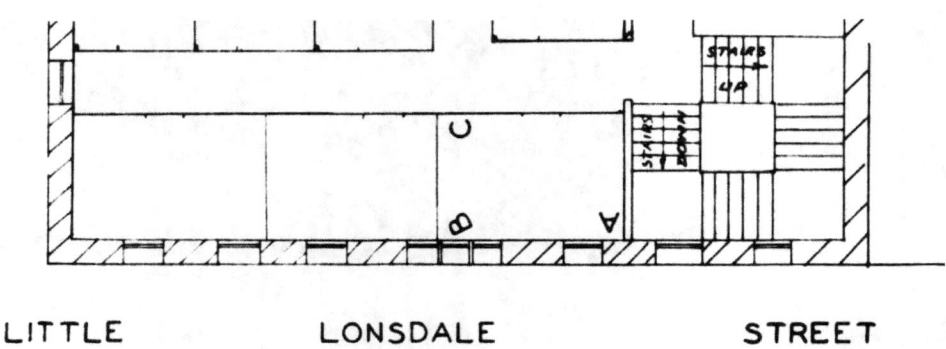

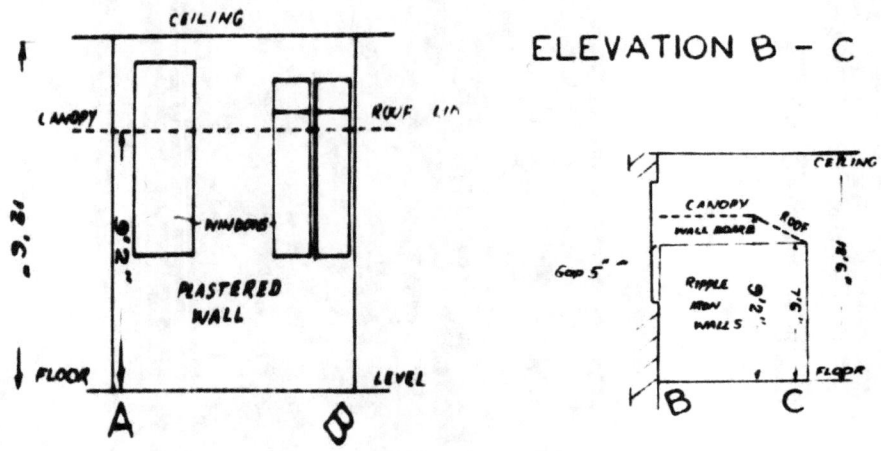

Plan Showing the Construction of Fox' Room
Coroner's Report

Reiger told Reid that no fuse was to be replaced until the following morning, as he personally wanted to investigate the cause. Reiger knew a likely cause was a heater or other illegal appliance being plugged in. If he waited, he could pinpoint the suspect who 'will be annoyed' but 'I can find out through the grapevine what caused the fuse to blow so that I can deal with it.' The strategy had worked before. Reid, embarrassed by his mistake, did not inform Reiger the fuse had already been replaced to no avail, it had blown not once, but twice.

～

It was then that a number of residents realised there was a problem. There was a simultaneous shout of FIRE!

Cannard, who was still examining the fuse box, raced down the passage to room 1 where he was met by two residents, one of whom was Mr Andrews. Andrews had been resting on his third floor bed when a friend yelled, 'A fire has broken out!' Andrews left his room to take a look. When he arrived at the end of the corridor, he could see smoke and a red glow under the bottom of the room 1 door. The fire, having been long contained, was attempting to break free of its confines.

Nightwatchman Kelvin Fitness was on the ground floor when he heard the commotion and went to investigate. Dashing to the third floor, he could see Fox's door still closed with the smoke entering the hall. He went to alert the sleeping men.

Fortuitously for Cannard, the fire equipment was right there with two residents ready to assist — Mr Andrews and a mate of his. Cannard pulled the firehose out, instructing Andrew's friend to 'bash down the door' to which he acknowledged 'all right.' Andrews reached for the hose tap but when he tried to turn it on 'it was too hot.' He jerked his hand away. The equipment appeared unusable.

As instructed, the door was smashed opened. This was a pivotal moment in the fire's progression and a critical error — the oxygen genie had been let out of the bottle and the dormant fire was given another lease of life. The fuel-rich air now exploded. Cannard later described the effect well, 'The fire seemed to me to be all bottled up.

The Fire Hose Lies where it was Dropped
Coroner's Report

Fox's Room was Obliterated
Coroner's Report

Immediately the door was opened, the flames came rushing out. I was on this side of the door and the other fellow was on the other side of the door. I could not see them for the flames.' The heat and blast generated by the backdraft was so intense that a fully kitted firefighter inside the room could not have survived. If Cannard or one of the residents had been standing at the door opening, they would have been blasted as if by a gigantic flamethrower and almost certainly killed.

Major Reiger and Booking Clerk Reid also arrived to investigate. They saw Andrews using the extinguisher but when it expelled the water[25] onto the flames it was useless — it was instantly vapourised in the inferno. They also noted the partially unwound hose that lay on the floor, where it had been dropped by Cannard.

THE WILLIAM BOOTH MEMORIAL HOME

The Fire in Full Flight
Fire Services Museum of Victoria

4th Floor Hallway Showing the Effects of the Superheated Upper Layer
Coroner's Report

Major Reiger could see the room was well ablaze and resident Andrews yelled out he could see someone lying on the cubicle floor. The sight that Andrews had seen was horrific. It looked like a body being consumed in a crematorium furnace. Flames were not coming out of the door, they had retreated after the initial rush, but they were all around the walls inside and incinerating the prostrate figure. Reiger later told the Coroner that he 'had only a quick look and tried to get in but it was impossible. I thought I would try the fire hose so I grabbed the nozzle of the fire hose and started to unwind it from around the pegs.' His aim was to suppress the fire near the prone man so he could be retrieved. However 'when the hose was unwound sufficiently I put my hand on the tap and received a shock. I thought it was electrified and it would be dangerous for anybody to touch it.' Reiger instructed those around him to leave it alone. Andrews made a last ditch attempt to reach the prone man but the heat, flames and smoke were unbearable. In any case Andrews could see the man was already 'well and truly gone.'

Reiger's assessment was correct that when the exposed wires had touched each other, the circuit had blown. It is unlikely that heat radiating from the fire had made the tap too hot to touch, as the water in the riser pipes would have absorbed any heat. It appears the metal riser or metal surround were electrified due to the corrupted circuit. It was a cruel irony — the firefighting equipment, just feet from the inferno, was unusable.

Then, to Reiger's amazement, he witnessed another spectacular display, 'All of a sudden, just before I rushed downstairs, everything seemed to go whoosh — everything seemed to go up into complete flame.' Following the backdraft another fire show had occurred — a flashover. After the super-heated top layer had exploded, the temperature in the room had climbed to 600°C (1112°F), the temperature at which most objects will self-ignite. The fireball caused all exposed surfaces to flame spontaneously. The surface of everything flammable caught fire in an instant and the room exploded for a second time. The windows now broke and the flames reached out to the winter sky and licked up towards the fourth floor windows.

Ernest Reid noticed the walls bulging around the hose. The fire had escaped the room and had moved behind the stairwell wall. Major Reiger yelled for everyone to get out and stopped Reid from ascending to the fourth floor to warn of the potential danger. Everyone now 'fled for their lives.'

～

Reid and Reiger rushed to the ground floor and called the fire brigade. The delay in calling the brigade proved to be critical. If they had been notified when the door of room 1 was still closed it is likely that the fire would have been contained.

Major Reiger then broadcast a warning to the occupants over the building's loudspeaker system, 'There is a fire on the third floor, please make your way down the back stairs.' He repeated the broadcast five times and could hear his voice on the ground floor speaker. However, the majority heard nothing, for a number of reasons. Many were asleep and one of the lodgers was deaf. One man thought it was a joke, believing one of the residents was operating the paging system. It was only when he smelt smoke that he knew it was for real. There was no fire alarm system in the building. There did not have to be.

A Flashover
Jamie Novak

THE WILLIAM BOOTH MEMORIAL HOME

The Escape Stairs Showing Scattered Clothing Items
Coroner's Report

Kelvin Fitness tried to return to Fox's room but he could not get all the way up the stairwell. He could see that the door was open and the fire had accelerated in a matter of minutes. He thought he would have time to knock on all the doors but it lit up so quickly. Fitness frantically bashed on the doors bellowing, 'There's a fire!' but the cubicle doors were locked shut from the inside. Which rooms were empty? Which rooms had drunken or sleeping residents? Fitness could only guess. From many there was no response and as time literally was the difference between life and death — for himself and the borders — he had to rush to the next room.

~

With no fireproof door on the southern stairwell, the rampant flames and smoke had a ready-made chimney to the floors above. David Robertson, a war pensioner, was reading the paper in his fourth floor room when he heard yelling. He did not take that much notice thinking, 'Someone had gone berserk, that's not so uncommon here.' The calls were persistent so he decided to get up. Donning his dressing gown, he stepped into the hall and was almost knocked unconscious with the amount of smoke billowing up from the third floor. In the haze somebody shouted, 'Follow me or you'll burn to death.' He struggled down the corridor, bumping into people, being knocked over, but somehow managing to regain his feet. Robertson knew if he did not stand up, he would die in the passageway. Somehow, he made his way to the north stairwell, losing consciousness as he tumbled down the stairs. Someone picked him up and carried him out. He woke up in hospital with bruised ribs but grateful he had survived, not knowing who had pulled him out.[26]

The fire was also erupting laterally across the third floor. Fox's cubicle disintegrated, the corrugated iron walls buckling and collapsing into a twisted heap over Fox's melted torso. Cannard's adjoining room was fully exposed and suffered the same fate. The three rooms on the south wall fell like a pack of cards, no match for the rolling firestorm.

The smoke, described by the firefighters as an impenetrable black cloud as thick as treacle and one of hottest they ever encountered, surged down the third floor hallway. The men in the open cubicles had little time to react. The open mesh cubicle roofs allowed the toxic cloud to penetrate the rooms in seconds. Many rooms were padlocked from the inside, some were double locked — the men wasting precious seconds trying to open the bolts. Being elderly and lacking mobility, they did not stand a chance as the superheated murk descended towards the floor and suffocated the life from their fragile bodies. Many never woke up at all.

Above on the fourth floor Kenny Haywood was reading *Life* magazine in bed when he also heard a disturbance.[27] After a few minutes he got sick of the commotion and decided he was going to break up the fight. When he reached the head of the south stairs he saw flames shooting up the banisters from the third floor. The fire was reaching upwards with frightening speed. It had also broken through the windows on the

The Rooms Next to Fox's Fell like a Pack of Cards
Coroner's Report

fourth floor with the flames from the third floor windows curling into those above.

Retreating to the north Haywood ran down the hallway kicking at doors, rattling the walls and screeching for people to get out. Someone thought he was joking but he was never more serious in his life. Benny Lennard, one of Haywood's Metropolitan Hotel drinking mates, was sitting in bed and had just taken a sleeping pill when Haywood pounded

Most Men Were Caged with Cyclone Mesh Covering their Rooms
Coroner's Report

on his wall. Like many Lennard was not sure whether it was a prank but he drowsily grabbed his bag and got out. Haywood ran to the north stairs but realised not all had been roused. The smoke was 'solid and scorching'; it was so thick it blotted the lights out with visibility now down to nil.

Haywood found a torch and placed a damp towel around his head. Through the blackness he shouted 'Follow me!' to which some of the confused residents responded, but others did not. He opened a window and herded survivors towards the fresh air. Haywood heard a resident, Dave Hartley, screaming. Haywood stumbled over half a dozen lifeless forms before getting to Hartley. Hartley screamed at Haywood to lift him to the window, wailing 'Get me out, get me out!' Haywood told him not to panic but Haywood himself by now was feeling faint, his head dreamlike and swimming.[28]

The most insidious by-product of any fire is carbon monoxide: odourless, tasteless and colourless, it is the biggest killer in most building fires. When a fire burns in an enclosed area the oxygen level decreases to a point where the combustion is incomplete and carbon monoxide is created. Haemoglobin, in the body's red blood cells, is responsible for transporting oxygen around the body. However, carbon monoxide binds to haemoglobin 240 times tighter than oxygen and as a result, the victim will suffocate. Haywood's symptoms of dizziness and weakness were typical of carbon monoxide poisoning. It can quickly lead to death. Haywood stuck his own head out the window and sucked in the oxygen, enough to revive. In that moment he lost track of Hartley, who would never leave the William Booth alive.

Robert Brown was resting in his fourth floor room when the fire broke out, 'I was near the front of the building and the fumes overpowered me and I fainted. When I woke up I was in hospital. I don't know who saved me or how.'[29]

The smoke also penetrated the second floor. It was here William Insley, an invalid pensioner, had fallen asleep in the afternoon. He had also not believed the shouts of 'Fire!', but then smelt the smoke and fumes which 'nearly did me in.' He had a chest complaint and as soon as he got a lung full of smoke, he knew he would not last long. Insley fell down the stairs sustaining a neck injury. Someone dragged him out of the building, but when he reached the pavement, he passed out.[30]

Les Anderson, the home's cafeteria manager was in his fifth story room, when he heard the crackling of flames. He ran down to investigate and was met by a wall of fire. He raced back up the stairs to warn his wife who was the only woman in the building. Anderson could not 'remember how we got out. I just grabbed my wife and ran.' They were fortunate to escape the building unscathed.[31]

A police patrol duty car was stopped in King Street by a passing motorist with the frantic message that there was a fire on Little Lonsdale Street. Senior Constable John Webster, Constable Arthur and First

Constable Dillon sprinted to the William Booth in their 'wireless' car.[32] They were the first service personnel on scene and could see that the third and fourth floors were well alight. Webster radioed back to base and asked the message be relayed to the fire brigade.

The three policemen entered the front door. They obtained the master keys and ran up the steps to the first floor where they saw a dozen elderly men shuffling in the corridors. Webster asked them to leave but they declined, expressing concern for their belongings, to which Webster replied that 'your belongings would be useless if you die in the fire.' The men then moved towards the back stairs, but not before they locked their rooms. The reaction of these men is typical for many in a fire; the urgency is not understood and the threat often underestimated. The police team opened each first floor cubicle and instructed those in their beds to move.

Close Up of Floor in Fox's Room
Coroner's Report

Eastern Hills Metropolitan Fire Brigade Headquarters
Fire Services Museum of Victoria

At 8.45 pm, numerous telephone calls were received at the Metropolitan Fire Brigade Headquarters, only three-quarters of a mile away from the fire. Manually activated street fire alarms rang at the same time, having been tripped by passers-by. The fire had by now reached an advanced stage and could be seen by many people.[33] The Metropolitan Fire Brigade Headquarters housed a huge watch room with thermal, sprinkler and street alarms. Four men operated it 24 hours a day and they knew the board so well that they could almost tell what building it was when a street alarm came in.

Fire engines from Headquarters, Batman Street and Carlton turned out immediately. Six fire engines were always sent for a city fire, two from each station with the furthest only five kilometres from the William Booth. When the bell peals, firefighters get their gear on as soon as possible as the adrenalin surges. In this case, the firefighters had mounted the engines and were out in under a minute. There was one advantage with a late evening callout, there was light traffic.

While proceeding up Batman Street, the glow from a fire could be seen and firefighter Jack Barker sent radio word that a fire was showing up, which means in firefighting lingo that the fire was real. Travelling further along King Street Barker could see the full extent — two floors were well alight. Barker made another call for more assistance. Six engines would not be enough.

At 8.48 pm[34], as he approached the corner of Latrobe and William Streets, Assistant Chief Officer Gordon Geddes from Headquarters also reported that the 'job is showing up.' Chief Officer Jack Paterson who was at home on leave was notified. Paterson scrambled into his uniform and shot out the door.

Gordon Geddes and Wife
Barbara McCumisky

As the highest ranked officer on scene, Geddes took charge and ordered the hose carriage crew to run two hose lines from a double-headed hydrant, which he had spotted on arrival. He then hastened to the ground floor foyer and was met by a hostel staff member. Geddes confirmed that people were still trapped upstairs and immediately sent word back to headquarters that there were 'reports of people trapped in the building and maximum assistance required.' In all 24 units and 64 men from seven stations would attend the disaster, including many who came in from leave.

Geddes then asked if there were any millcocks in the

building and was directed to the one on the ground floor. This was a good sign. He knew if there was one on the ground floor there must be hydrants on the upper floors. This meant the fire could be attacked from an internal water supply as well as the external hydrants. Geddes went to the front door and yelled, 'I want men here at once!' Two men responded, Trevor Reed and Alby Hall.[35] Fireman Reed had arrived on a combination ladder engine and as the engine had turned into Little Lonsdale Street, Reed had instructed the driver to the front of the building so the ladder would be available.

Once firefighter Barker and his team arrived, they ran out lines of hose and directed them on to the fire from the roadway.[36] With the front stairs covered by Geddes and his crew, Barker, accompanied by Sub-Station Officer Ernie Scown and Fireman Peter Wade, made for the stairs to the north.[37]

Trevor Reed
Trevor Reed

Alby Hall
Barbara McCumisky

Heavy debris was raining on the stairway from above as firefighters Reed and Hall ran up the south stairs. Reed made it to the third floor but could go no further. The floor was well alight so he retreated to the level below, rousing residents by kicking on doors and yelling for the men to get out.

When Assistant Chief Officer Geddes reached the third floor, he made a quick assessment; he believed the fire could be hit and extinguished with a single line of hose from the inside. Reed and Hall ran a line from the second floor hydrant.

The two firefighters attached a line; they always worked in pairs to back each other up. The hose, on a figure of eight bollard, rolled out easily but it had a tendency to kink which had to be removed. Laid and then turned on, the hose delivered a powerful torrent of water, attacking the flames head on. The heat was unbelievable, with the water on the ceiling reaching boiling point and burning Reed's ungloved hands as it dripped down off the ceiling.

On reaching the north third floor landing, a resident told firefighter Scown that some men were still trapped. Scown carefully opened the third floor fire door. It was not fully closed as the self-closing spring was broken and the door scraped on the floor. The door could therefore not function as designed.

There were five men in a semi-conscious and unconscious state inside the door. Wade and Scown removed them to the landing but there was a problem. There was a lack of manpower to move them down. Firefighter Barker did his best with policeman Webster and his colleagues assisting.

Ernie Scown
Fire Services Museum of Victoria

THE WILLIAM BOOTH MEMORIAL HOME

A Leyland Metz Ladder attended the Conflagration
Barbara McCumisky

When Station Officer Roy Treverton (No 1 Station Hose Carriage) entered the hostel, he noticed a number of civilians either leaving through the main entrance or milling in the foyer. He immediately ordered them to vacate the building.[38] He was met by Booking Clerk Reid who informed Treverton that there were men trapped on the third floor. Treverton entered the lift with Reid, but when they reached the third floor, the lift door only opened a few inches and refused to budge. Through the crack, they could see flames and smoke directly in front of them, funnelling to the upper floors. They were in a death trap, in grave danger of being baked to death in the tiny booth. In desperation Treverton jammed his foot in the door opening and with brute strength, pushed the door open. Using a lift in a fire was an elementary error, but luckily they were not casualties. He ordered Reid to return to the ground floor by the stairway.

Treverton saw two men trying to reach the stairs. One was Reg Deacon who had a crippled left leg. While in bed someone had opened the door and shouted out 'Reg, you'd better get slipping, the place is on fire!' There were heavy fumes and smoke coming in gusts so he did not have time to put the callipers on his leg. Deacon hobbled down the corridor, leaning on the wall. Someone ran completely over the top of him causing him to crumple to the floor.[39] Treverton, assisted by firefighter Ivan Nunn, carried him downstairs.[40]

∼

Another problem was ambulance availability as the emergency services were overwhelmed. Forty-two people perished in Victoria over this August weekend, including eight in road accidents and four in a plane crash.[41] It was some time before the paramedics arrived at the William Booth. The firemen set up a first aid post on the ground floor and with no ambulance personnel available it was up to the firefighters to perform resuscitation. For fireman Gray it was not a pleasant task. The old men had saliva and body fluids running out of their mouths and nose, most of them were smoke stained and unconscious, some had no dentures and alcohol was prevalent. No one liked the idea of placing their mouths on the victims. Firefighter Lionel Sleeman had a solution. He yelled out, 'Pull your handkerchief out, place it over their mouth and start working!' Mouth-to-mouth resuscitation was in its infancy and few men knew how to apply it. After attempting it Gray reverted to the Silvester manual resuscitation method, laying the patients on their backs, raising their arms above the head and then pressing them against the chest to force respiration.[42]

Like a scene from a warzone, bodies were sprawled all over the ground floor corridor. If the man was deemed dead, he was dragged into the makeshift mortuaries, one in the dining room and the other in the lounge. There was no other place available to store the corpses. A photographer, Ken Rainsbury, arrived and captured the despair. The dead men were laid out in rows. On occasion one of those believed to be dead would move or cry out and the firefighters would re-attend to them.[43]

A young reporter, Jeff Penberthy, also arrived. He watched the resuscitation attempts and saw two exhausted firefighter lugging a 14

Les Gray Resuscitating a Victim using the Silvester Method. Station Officer Jack Barker is Directly Behind Gray.
Les Gray

stone body down the smoke-drenched stairs.[44] Due to the build-up of heat, the victims' bodies were sweating profusely making it almost impossible for one man to bring them out of the building, their pyjamas and clothing coming off them like overripe bananas. The firefighters soon found that working in pairs was the quickest and easiest method to retrieve the victims. The back one supported the victim under the arms, the front one held their legs, the fore-and-aft method. When only a single helper was available, they were dragged down the stairs backwards.[45] The carriage of bodies to the resuscitation zone on the ground floor lasted an hour.

A Victim Being Carried by the Fore-and-Aft Method
Les Gray

Reporter Penberthy saw the desperation in the firefighters. 'Come on, live!' was the desperate plea of a brigade member as he worked on one of the men. The expression on the man's face said it all. The number of dead and dying was incomprehensible and overwhelming. The firefighters were trained to fight fires, not to resuscitate dozens of dying men. When the ambulances finally arrived, the men gave thanks — it had seemed like an eternity. A St John ambulance officer spread the scarce supplies of oxygen amongst the ailing men. Major Reiger asked for more blankets. With sufficient ambulance and policemen now in attendance, the firemen were free for search and removal work, but only once the fire was under control.

A Fireman Being Relieved by an Ambulance Officer
Les Gray

Back on the third floor, Assistant Chief Officer Geddes and his crew had found themselves confronted with an impassable wall of fire. They directed the water stream into the heart of the blaze, attempting to quell it so rescue operations could be carried out. By this time, other hoses had been run up the front stairs to supplement the hose from the second floor hydrant. After five minutes of a continuous torrent, Geddes felt the fire was coming under control. This was 19 minutes after the first call. With the stairs now passable Geddes went to check the fourth floor.

Smoke conditions on the fourth floor were abysmal. One fireman had ripped off the wire mesh covering the windows to open them in an attempt to allow the smoke and hot gases to escape (vent). Geddes had no choice but to crawl, inching along and calling loudly, 'Is there anyone there?' He received muffled replies and called out for the victims to follow his light. The hand torches were 6-volt battery acid type, which soon ran down. They had little reach in the black hole that was the third and fourth floor. One man stumbled past to the stairs and Geddes helped another. This was his first definite knowledge that men were trapped on the fourth. As Geddes received no further response, he returned to the third floor and found additional men arriving. With the fire in control, the focus switched to recovery but although the flames had receded, the smoke conditions were still treacherous and there was only one solution.

Geddes called for all Proto breathing apparatus men to prepare for searching. The Proto was a type of 'rebreather', a closed circuit breathing

Frantic revival Attempts in the Hallway. Makeshift Mortuaries were Established in the Adjoining Dining and Lounge Rooms
Salvation Army

apparatus with oxygen cylinders. Within the next five minutes, Firefighter Nunn appeared clad in the equipment. Able to breathe but with low visibility he forced a way along the north-south passage and looked for more victims on the third floor. Within minutes he returned to advise that 'they are up at the other end.' He could see bodies to the north.

~

Firefighters Wade and Scown had initially tried to move up the third floor passage from the north to south but were driven back by smoke. Visibility was nil and headway could only be made by crawling and kneeling on the floor, groping along with extended arms, feeling cautiously with the back of hands.

With Scown and Wade unable to make headway, Scown told Wade to get him a Proto. He returned ready, had a rope line attached and was joined by Laurie Lavelle who had also donned the breathing apparatus. Together they went into the floor and within a short distance had found the body Nunn had seen from the other end. The man was removed to the landing. They went to investigate the nearby cubicles but could find no other victims. They missed the toilet section, directly opposite the faulty fire door, and moved to the fourth floor and found yet more bodies in the passage.

Policemen Webster and Arthur had been working in the fourth floor shower room. The smoke, soot laden, was so thick Webster vomited on two occasions and then dry retched. The policemen smashed more windows, gulped down breaths of fresh air and grabbed whomever they could. There were many men inside. The Proto crew of Wade and Lavelle arrived and assisted in the removals. Wade and Lavelle then moved back to the third.

The Dire Conditions the Policemen Rescuers Faced in the Showers
Coroner's Report

By this time Chief Officer Paterson had arrived. He was beloved by the men, a firefighter's fireman. His presence always lifted morale for he knew everybody by name. Some men lead by example and Paterson was one of them, always at the front line, putting his life on the line. He now took charge from Geddes.

As the crews with breathing gear moved in from both sides of the third floor, there was the most gruesome find of all. Just opposite the northern fire door was the combined shower-toilet block, which had been missed in the initial search. Like the fourth floor above, the confused men had taken a wrong turn at the end of the corridor. In the chaos, they had reached the fire door but instead of turning right, they had shuffled to the left, become disorientated and trapped. The area was full of bodies, the barely living entangled with the dead. Some had turned the showers on, some put towels on their heads, anything that might aid survival. Up to a dozen lifeless bodies were dragged out, mouths gaping open, in a death stare. Their soot shadows remained on the floor, like ghostly etches on a canvas. Remarkably, there were survivors. Lavelle observed one of the men shuffling around like a zombie, face black with soot. Police and firefighters combined to get the mostly lifeless men out and down the back stairs as quickly as possible. A full-scale room-by-room search on the third and fourth floors was then undertaken.

Although both corridors had by now been searched, no side passages and cubicles had. Back on the southern end of the third floor, Reed secured a rope line to Treverton, who with Proto support carried out a search of the floor. He returned in a short time with an unconscious person and assisted in carrying the victim to the ground floor. Men were found in various positions; under beds, across beds, slumped near and behind doors. The toll was mounting. The last deceased was found under a bed where he had sought protection, well after previous searches had been undertaken in the same room. The conditions had been that dire.

William Insley, the resident who had escaped from the second floor, regained consciousness on the ground outside the building. He saw

Chief Officer Jack Paterson
Fire Services Museum of Victoria

firefighters plying hoses on the fire as great pieces of glass fell from the upper floor windows and shattered on the concrete below. The ground was awash with water, the streams from the hoses combining with the freezing August rain. Although the fire was out, he could see thick black plumes still coming from the front and side windows with the brick walls significantly blackened. Insley crawled over the road where a man covered him with a blanket. When he woke up in hospital, he was told he had been marked as DOA (Dead on Arrival). He had passed out for a second time.[46]

Carnage in the Shower.
A Death Soot Shadow is Seen in the Photo Below (left)
Coroner's Report

THE WILLIAM BOOTH MEMORIAL HOME

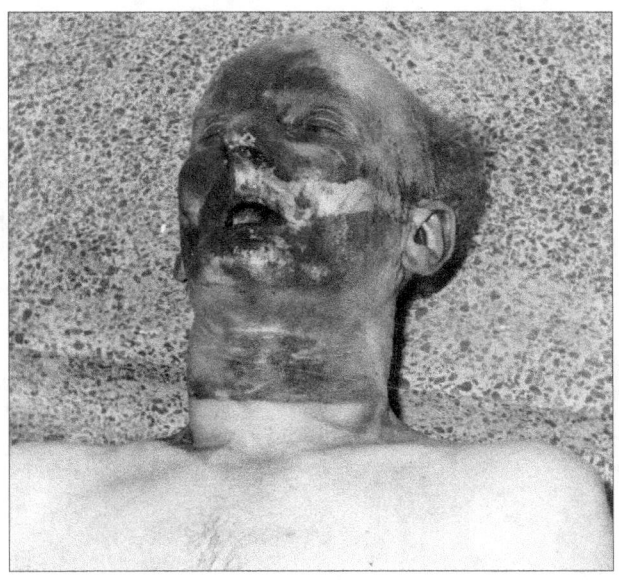

More Death Soot Shadows are Seen in the Photo Above.
Below is a Victim
Coroner's Report

Outside the William Booth, firefighters propped up the rescued along the walls as they waited for ambulances. Those residents who had escaped stood outside, lost and disorientated and smoking in the steady rain. The injured and dying were relayed to the Royal Melbourne, St Vincent's, Prince Henry's and Alfred hospitals. The mortuary could not cope; bodies were distributed to hospitals until the backlog was dealt with.[47] The survivors, approximating 150, were accommodated at the Gill Memorial home, the Salvos People's Palace and homes of Salvation Army officers. There were so many they had to doss down on the floor, head to tail.

With Paterson now leading the clean-up operation, they were able to enter Fox's cubicle in room 1 on the third floor. It had been obliterated in the heat, only the twisted metal walls still visible and the remainder of Fox, now but a torso, burnt beyond recognition. He looked 'just like

Firemen Propping Up the Victims Outside
Salvation Army

a flounder with all the bones removed.' After the fire had 'flashed over' and all objects in the room auto-ignited, the temperature climbed to over 1000°C (1850°F). The effect on Fox's body was devastating, the skin reddening and blistering, the muscles and limb tendons contracting with the arms grotesquely raised as if to punch (known as the Pugilistic Pose). The skin had shrunk exposing the bones. Most of his legs and much of his torso was consumed in the fire with the ribs exposed. He lost half of his body weight. The smell of burnt flesh was overpowering.

The fire inspectors set about determining the cause. Fox was on his back, next to the upturned heater. When and how did he die? Clues were revealed in the autopsy.

A 5cm by 1cm extradural brain haemorrhage was noted on the back of his head. If this was the case it would be an artefact of the fire, the extreme heat cooking bone marrow tissue. The medical examiner then switched his reference to a subdural haemorrhage, a different beast altogether where a 'bridging vein' (a blood vessel near the surface of the brain) has torn. A subdural haemorrhage is caused by blunt force trauma until proven otherwise.[48] This could have happened through a previous fall and may have developed over several weeks. It has been well established that alcoholics are at an increased risk of developing a subdural bleed in falls.

Fox had soot in the lungs which meant he was breathing after the fire had started. It was also established that Fox died early in the fire because his carbon monoxide level was zero. As the room had no ventilation the

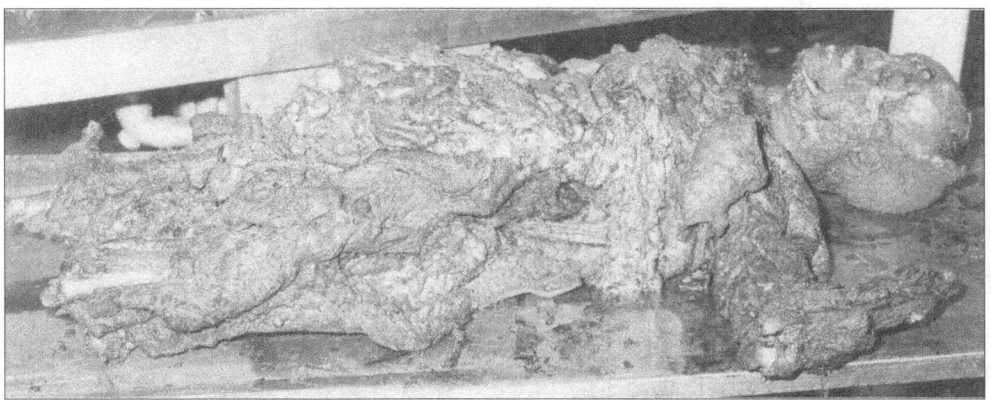

The Devastating Effects of a Flashover and Backdraft on the Body of Fox
Coroner's Report

carbon monoxide levels would have risen quickly, although more slowly at floor level where he was lying. Some time after knocking the heater he may have noticed the incipient fire and responded. A heart attack is a distinct possibility, especially if he was exposed to the flame. His significant heart disease meant he was primed for cardiac arrhythmia and subsequent cardiac arrest. Soot from the upper layers of the room would have drifted down into Fox's lungs as he took his last breaths, dying from a heart attack. If he had an extradural and subdural haemorrhage (and this is unclear in the report), the subdural haemorrhage pressing on the brain may have impeded his capacity to respond to the fire. The effects of alcohol would have further compounded his ability to react to the danger. It is also possible Fox had a heart attack, knocked the heater over when he collapsed, and finally died of the attack after the fire had started.[49]

Reed, Chief Paterson and two other firefighters looked over the remains. They put his body onto a tarpaulin, using two square mouth shovels. Although he had been a heavy man, much of his body had disappeared and his removal proved a light task. Paterson then sent word back to headquarters that the situation was under control. The time was 9.45 pm, an hour after the initial alert.

Four firefighters were slightly injured fighting the fire; one suffered concussion when he struck his head on a stairway while carrying an unconscious man to safety. He was taken to hospital, but returned to the fire after treatment. The other main casualty was Deputy Chief Fire Officer Frank Tueno who was hit in the face with a jet of water from a hose line and was taken to St. Vincent's Hospital with particles of grit in his eyes.

~

Twenty-five men lost their lives in the fire and five more died later. Half were from the third floor and half from the fourth with carbon monoxide the biggest killer. The final victim was Frederick Haas. He was admitted to hospital with superficial burns but with severe bronchospasm. He was given antibiotics, steroids, bronchodilators, diuretics and analgesics. As a last ditch effort, due to his deteriorating respiratory condition, a tracheotomy was performed. Haas' status subsequently improved but he developed cardiac arrhythmia and eventually succumbed.

THE WILLIAM BOOTH MEMORIAL HOME

Above: Ambulance Officers in front of the Leyland Metz Rescue Ladder

Below: Scenes of Despair Outside the William Booth

Salvation Army

Most of the survivors returned to the William Booth the next day in replacement clothes given to them by the Salvos. They were still dazed and puffed on cigarettes for comfort. The men waited outside, before being led in small groups into the Home, searching their meagre belongings, knowing they could not return until a decision was made on the building's future. For many the William Booth had been their home for years and the loss of their only friend, the comfort of its routine and its familiarity, was the most traumatic effect of the fire.

The men were watched by a small group of curious sightseers. On re-entering the building, nightwatchman Fitness eyed the desolation in the gutted third floor corridor but remarkably found his cornet intact, only covered in a thick layer of soot. One man returned to look for his prized possession, a charred bible. His life savings were inside, 90 dollars untouched.[50]

There were difficulties in identifying the bodies due to the men's reclusiveness and because some had used multiple aliases. The name of a friend on a tattered Christmas card, an address on a doctor's prescription, initials on a photograph — these mementos helped identify the dead.[51] The Salvos received numerous gifts for the survivors through several private appeals. The manager of the home, Brigadier Barry, received gifts of money and clothes from private citizens. 'We are also going to be a bit short on blankets, linen and mattresses, but I urge anyone wanting to donate anything like this to first contact our headquarters in Bourke Street', he said.[52] One schoolboy sent a letter to the Salvos which said 'I did not know before that the Salvation Army cared for poor people like this, and I am sending the contents of my money box ($1.04).'[53]

Fifteen of the deceased remained unclaimed by relatives with the Salvos 'accepting the responsibility' of the funeral arrangements. It was held in the City Temple, Bourke Street, on 23 August 1966. Fire Chief Paterson told firefighters Reed and Treverton that he wanted them to represent the Melbourne Fire Brigade at the remembrance service. They marched with the funeral cortege up Bourke Street and sat in the City Temple, 15 coffins laid out in a row. Reed remembers this as the saddest part of the whole tragedy. Four hundred mourners attended but only the staff had known the deceased. The nobodies were laid to rest.

THE WILLIAM BOOTH MEMORIAL HOME

Funeral March
Salvation Army

Funeral Procession
Salvation Army

The Nobodies are Laid to Rest
Salvation Army

Smoke inhalation and carbon monoxide poisoning have always been hazards of the job for firefighters and even as late as 1966, firefighters had little protection against its damaging effects. After the William Booth fire, the fire brigade purchased compressed air breathing apparatus sets and firefighters gradually came to accept the wearing of breathing apparatus as a normal part of the job.[54]

Another change was in the teaching of mouth-to-mouth resuscitation. Fireman Gray recalls, 'After that fire we did drill after drill after drill on it. We ended up knowing it like the Lord's Prayer.'

The fire protection requirements of the Booth, a 'lodging house' were determined by the Department of Health's Fire Prevention Regulations of 1949. By law, the building needed a fire service and extinguishers (properly maintained) and a proper alternative means of escape. All of these requirements were met. It did not require alarms and sprinklers. It was estimated it would have cost $12,000 to install sprinklers in the Booth, money the Salvation Army did not have. A charitable

THE WILLIAM BOOTH MEMORIAL HOME

THE SALVATION ARMY

IN SOLEMN REMEMBRANCE

Order of Services

For the Funeral of

VICTIMS OF THE TRAGIC FIRE WHICH OCCURRED AT THE WILLIAM BOOTH MEMORIAL HOSTEL FOR MEN ON SATURDAY, AUGUST 13th, 1966

Conducted by

COMMISSIONER HUBERT R. SCOTNEY

at the

Melbourne City Temple, Tuesday, August 23rd, 1966, at 2.30 p.m.,

and privately at the Fawkner Crematorium.

organisation, the Salvos were barely managing to cover the running costs of the much needed establishment.

The Government ordered reports from the fire brigade, Health Department and police. The Victorian Premier Sir Henry Bolt said the government would not comment until it had received reports from the fire brigade and the Salvation Army, commenting, 'everyone is stunned by this shocking tragedy.' The Leader of the Opposition said, 'Whenever a dreadful holocaust of this kind has happened in the past and it has mostly been in the distant past, the outraged public has demanded drastic reforms to prevent a similar tragedy. Everyone is shocked that such a thing is possible in Australia in 1966.'[55]

The William Booth had become — and remains — Australia's deadliest building fire. Apart from the thirty deaths, the fire also dealt a mortal blow to the William Booth as a lodging house. The Salvation Army could not meet the costs of repairs. In 1967, it was sold to a private company of Melbourne businessmen. The doors were closed on 16 December 1967 and it was eventually demolished.[56]

The last word can be left to the Victorian coroner: 'We all know the Salvation Army does a wonderful job in caring for destitute and homeless men but, at the time, this building was not *sprinklered* (author's emphasis). Let's hope that with the modern fire protection and fire prevention practices and legislation, this type of fire should never occur again in Australia.'

The coroner would be dismayed that 163 people have died in building fires since 1966 (see Appendix 1), all in buildings that did not have sprinklers. Seven of these were in another Salvo lodging house in Adelaide in 1975.

The People's Palace

Adelaide

22 April 1975

It had been a night of celebration. The Congress Hall had hosted a hearty concert featuring the band of the fourth military district. The pre-Anzac Accolade ceremony entertained 300 enthusiastic patrons until 9.30 pm. The hall was vacated and inspected by the bandleader at 10.30 pm. All the doors and windows were checked and secured.

The People's Palace in Adelaide was originally a German club and comprised two distinct areas. At the rear was the huge single storey Congress Hall replete with (from west to east) a gallery (with one hundred chairs), main seating, performance stage and youth hall. The Congress Hall was reputedly the first Salvation Army 'Citadel' built in Australia.[57] In an elevated alley, 20 feet above the youth hall, there was accommodation for 12 men. Known as 'the Tipperary', it was named after the Irish village. The front of the building included the main entrance, administration area, kitchen and on the upper two levels, lodging for singles to families of six.

Like the William Booth Memorial Home, the Palace complied with all fire legislation. The 19 extinguishers and six hose reels had been inspected a year previously by the fire brigade and were in top working order. Curiously in 1966, the fire brigade had recommended that fire warning devices be installed and the public address system upgraded. Was this a response to the William Booth Hostel fire in Melbourne? Regardless, the upgrade was not mandated and did not occur.

∼

Just before 9.45 pm a young lady entered the People's Palace and requested Mr Allen, her former fiancé, be paged. Brett Allen, a resident in the Tipperary, made his way to the foyer.[58] Allen had recently arrived from Perth, coincidentally on the same Greyhound bus as another

Tipperary resident. Allen talked for a time and disappeared. The day watchman, Mr Day, was suspicious.[59] The Tipperary was a strictly men's only area, with no lady visitors allowed. Day decided to investigate. He made his way to Allen's room but before knocking listened to make sure he could hear two voices. His suspicion was correct. Day rapped on the door and asked, 'Have you a young lady in here?' to which Allen responded, 'Yes we are talking.' Day was firm, 'This is not allowed, you can talk in the TV or writing room but ladies are not permitted in here.' Allen escorted his former fiancée to the front door where she left by taxi and then Allen returned to his room.

Day's replacement, Harold Doyle, the night porter and watchman arrived at 10.00 pm for a 10.30 pm start.[60] He was a general rouseabout with duties including cleaning, bookings and like Fitness at the William Booth, keeping a watchful eye over the building. During the night Doyle was kept busy, attending the books, doing his inspections and unlocking the front door to let in the occasional late returning lodger.

One was William Simm who returned to the Palace at 2.00 am. Mr Simm was formerly a taxi driver in Darwin who had left after the devastation of Cyclone Tracy. He had driven his white Holden cab all the way to Adelaide. For three months, he had been operating on a restricted license but had just received his full South Australian license. Even better he was to start work with an Adelaide taxi company that very day.[61] Things were on the up as he made his way to bed in the Tipperary, he would need a good sleep for his upcoming shift.

Like all catastrophic building fires, it was peaceful at the Palace just before the inferno broke. Everything changed at the devil's hour, 3.00 am.

∼

At 3.10 am Doyle was sitting in the booking office when he thought he could smell smoke. He was instantly alert with fear. Nothing made Doyle more nervous than fire and he was acutely aware of such a danger. His brother has been horribly burnt to death.

Following his nose he went across the foyer, through the dining room and out to the kitchen. He could see nothing untoward so he ascended to the first floor and made for the TV room. There was a heater which he thought might have fallen over. All was in order. To his left he turned

THE PEOPLE'S PALACE

The People's Palace
Coroner's Report

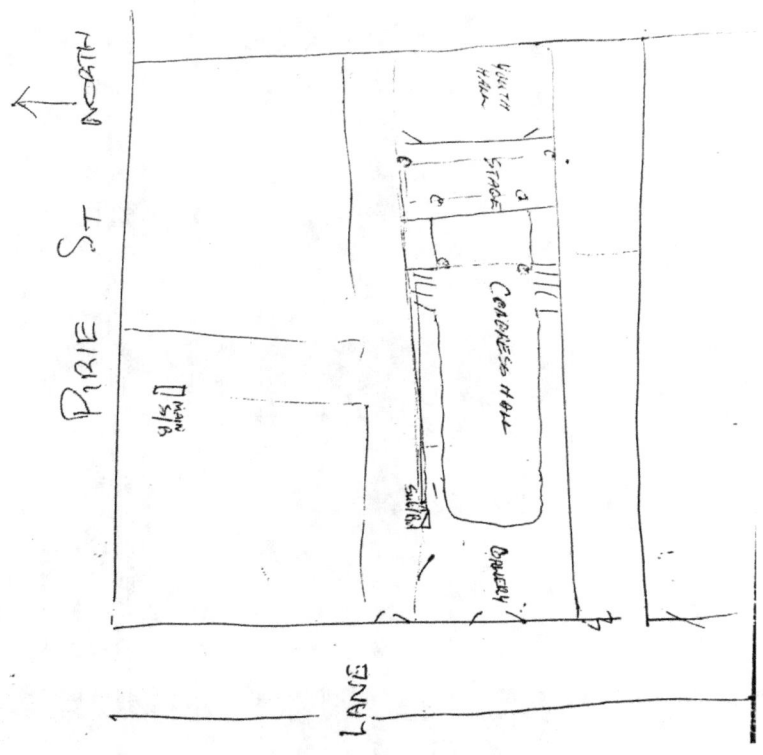

Sketch Map of the Congress Hall
Coroner's Report

up the passage, leading towards the Tipperary. He had only walked a few paces when he could hear running footsteps. Two men tore past yelling, 'There's a fire, there's a fire!' The men had come from room 59 in the south-west corner. One had been reading in bed when he heard a noise resembling a 'rumbling jet'. He could smell smoke, jumped to the window and could see flames shooting up.[62] Doyle gave the men the front door keys and asked them to ring the fire brigade.

Doyle came to a south facing window that overlooked the Congress Hall and it was then he could see it. Flames and smoke were billowing out of the Hall to the west and centre, although none were over the Tipperary accommodation, to the east.

He knocked on the door of room 58 and told the occupant to leave, then proceeded to all the other rooms in the vicinity completing a sweep of the top floor. He repeated the effort on the middle level. The people were leaving slowly, wanting to pack their belongings before they left.

Strangely, it was only then he arrived at the entrance to the Tipperary corridor, ten minutes after having initially seen the fire. This area was the section closest to the fire, being elevated above the Congress Hall. Just outside the corridor entrance was a Fire Escape sign pointing south. He knew the area well as in the past he had boarded in a Tipperary room. At the far end of the corridor, he could make out the light on in the bathroom and through the dense haze he could just see the southern wall fire escape. The wooden escape door led to the street below but it was locked.

He knew this because he had checked it himself. When Doyle first started his role, one of his duties was to check that the southern exit door was secured so that 'the undesirables' were kept out. On occasion, non-guests, sometimes under the influence, had gained access to the Palace during the night. It was left unlocked by day. There were in fact two doors, one a fly wire door that was pulled inwards (spring loaded) and which locked automatically. It could be opened from the inside. The outer wooden door opened outwards and required a key, a key that was kept in the booking office in slot 83. In addition, the door had a Yale lock with a slip catch. Conscious of the death of his brother Doyle had been disturbed by the practice and had asked the previous manager of the Palace about the possibility of fire. Doyle was told, 'It wouldn't be too much trouble breaking it down.' Locking the fire escape door had been a security practice for at least five years.

Night watchman Doyle could see the smoke was heavy in the Tipperary corridor but no flames were obvious. He was able to move a third of the way up and knocked on a couple of doors shrieking, 'Fire!', but then retreated as he could not breathe.

Lodger Allen was asleep in room 34, halfway down the Tipperary. He woke up when he felt part of the ceiling hit him on the shoulder. 'I realised there was plenty of smoke so I jumped out of bed, and I raced up to the door, I turned on the light and the room was completely filled with smoke. I opened up the door, stumbled back, felt my clothes underneath my feet, I picked those up and got to the door, then for a quick second I didn't know if the front of the building was on fire or the back so I decided to go to the fire escape door.'

The smoke was impenetrable and he could not see his outstretched hands. When he arrived at the fire exit, he found it was locked. Allen pushed on it, throwing all his 12.5 stone (79 kilograms) behind it.

Above: Foyer of the Congress Hall
Below: Entrance to the Congress Hall from the Administration Area.
Likely Access Point for an Arsonist
Coroner's Report

However, it would not budge and he did not have time to keep trying. He turned round and went down the passageway to the north (which led to the main entrance), bumping into two other people on the way. He exited the People's Palace out the front door.

Mr Berryman was asleep in room 26 of the Tipperary. He was awoken by people running around. He looked at his digital clock, it was 3.30 am. He could see smoke coming up between the floorboards in the room; he leaped from bed, opened the door and, like Allen, fled down the northern corridor. He was the last to get out alive.

Smoke was now starting to penetrate the main accommodation area of the Palace. Mrs Hovath, after hearing banging on the door and yelling, fled down the stairs with her purse her only possession. In the melee at the front entrance of the building, a man ran past and snatched her handbag. She later found her handbag but $300 was missing. For one man the fire had been an opportunity.[63]

A lady and child sleeping on the top floor in room 66 were lucky to escape. It was the only room in the main body severely damaged by fire with the windows completely burnt away as well as part of the bed.

Aerial View of the Gutted Congress Hall
Coroner's Report

The police were the first to arrive, Doyle saw them standing at the bottom of the stairs leading to the Tipperary. 'You fellows got here real quick', he remarked. 'Yes we were cruising down Pulteney Street and Police Headquarters notified us', was the response. They asked if any people were in the Tipperary. Doyle said some were booked in but he was unsure if they were still in the section. There were in fact ten rooms occupied that night and only three of the occupants escaped.

The first call to the fire brigade was received at 3.26 am, up to a staggering 16 minutes after Doyle had detected the smoke.[64] They were there in a minute. A hose carriage, salvage and combination engine with

Gutted Congress Hall
Coroner's Report

a total of three officers and eight firefighters responded. There was then a quick request for two additional fire engines. Fires hoses were run to the back of the Congress Hall.

When the firefighters arrived at the Tipperary at 3.32 am, two minutes after the last survivor had fled, the smoke was so extreme that breathing apparatus would be required. A lifeline was attached to Officer Charles Amey so he could retrace steps. He was scouting ahead for the breather team. He went about 12 feet down, visibility was minimal and it was intensely hot. Amey went into one room on the right, put the light on, no one was there. He then went back into the passage but the ceiling was giving way in small chunks with embers drifting down. It was time to beat a hasty retreat. It was too late for a rescue.[65]

As Amey stepped out of the Tipperary corridor into the People's Palace, he told the fire crew it 'is going to go in minutes.' At that instant the ceiling of the Tipperary collapsed, closely followed by the remainder of the alley. The conditions were so dire the firefighters could only hear the structure smash onto the floor of the Congress Hall, they could not see it. Had they gone in five minutes earlier they would been lost themselves.

The fire was not declared under control until 4.21 am. The Congress Hall was obliterated with fire damage only to rooms 58 and 66 and superficial and smoke damage to the main body of the People's Palace.

Eighty-nine people had fled in their nightclothes. They were accommodated at the Governor Hotel with the nearby YMCA giving them a breakfast. Four people including three children were taken to hospital for smoke inhalation.[66]

Seven bodies were found amongst the charred and twisted beams and debris under what had been the Tipperary. Four of the men had alcohol readings ranging from 0.08 to 0.12. Five men were found near the south-east corner and two on the eastern side, a third of the way from the southern end. Superintendent Desmond Panizza, a veteran fire inspector concluded the Tipperary floor had tilted to the west and north.[67] As the men lived in the northern rooms this indicated they were congregated at the southern exit and had been overcome with carbon monoxide. The dead men had lethal levels of carbon monoxide ranging from 46 to 76 per cent. The conclusion was the men had been trapped at the southern exit door, unable to break through the locked exit. There they had died and then fallen when the structure collapsed.

Above: Floor of the Fallen Tipperary Section
Below: Close Up of Furniture Items from the Tipperary Rooms
Coroner's Report

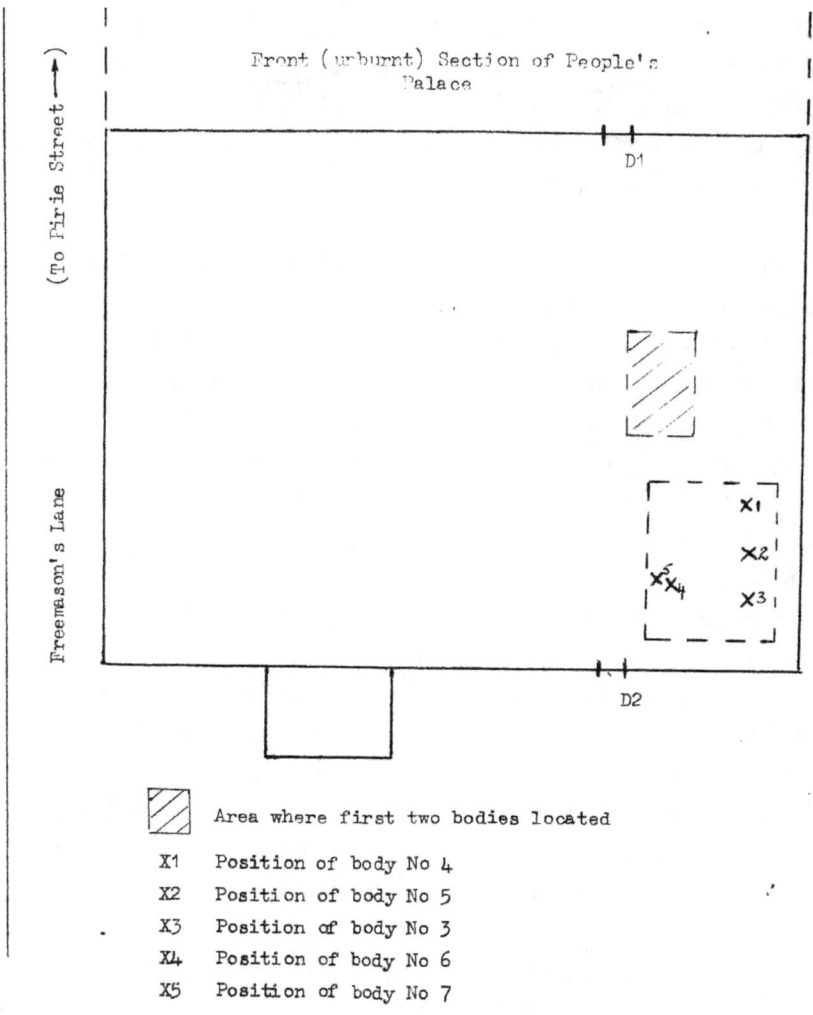

Sketch Diagram of Bodies Under the Tipperary Exit Which was Locked
Coroner's Report

It was clear the fire started in the western section of the Congress Hall and under the gallery area. Large areas of the floor had been completely destroyed and large areas of masonry spalling (flaking) revealed a 'low burning pattern'. This pattern was suspicious as the area under the gallery had little to sustain a fire (concrete and non-flammable carpet), which suggested the use of an accelerant. An intense fire over a large area had been initiated in this location, but how?

The first suspect was new electrical cabling that had been installed that very day. Cables had been run from the switchboard area to above the stage but the cables had not been connected, they carried no current. In any case, the stage was towards the east away from the point of origin. Other electrical appliances were examined and tested, and quickly ruled out.

The next possibility was a cigarette butt. A number of the concert band members smoked but they did so in the youth room under the Tipperary, again at the opposite end from the gallery. Was a cigarette in the main hall the source? Thousands of dollars of new carpets and furniture had been installed only a week before in the aisles between the seats. A lighted cigarette was held against a new piece of carpet and it failed to burn. The seats were covered in vinyl. Could a cigarette have been caught in a seating fold? This was deemed unlikely but could not be ruled out.

Superintendent Panizza believed it was arson. There were several possible points of entry for a pyromaniac: a sash window in the south-west corner, a door entrance from the People's Palace or a louver window at the ground floor west. The sash was intact and the louver only had a bend on one pane. The simplest and most likely access point was the door from the People's Palace and therefore an inside job. If it was arson, then the next questions were who and why. At the coroner's inquest one witness was probed repeatedly, Mr Allen, because of inconsistencies in his story.

At one stage Allen had told a journalist his girlfriend had visited at 10.00 pm. When Day told her to leave, they went straight to the foyer, rang for a taxi and they both left the Palace with Allen only returning at 1.30 am. When cross-examined at the coroner's inquest Allen concurred there was a discrepancy but mused he may have been referring to the night before. With a lack of evidence the coroner had to conclude Allen may have been genuinely confused and not seeking payback for the 10.00 pm rebuke, when his former fiancée had been expelled from the premises.

Another motive given for arson was the visit of the Salvation World Leader, General Wiseman, who was due to arrive at the Palace on 26 April,[68] just days after the Congress Hall was gutted. There was no evidence to support this hypothesis nor, in the end, was there enough evidence to charge anyone. The coroner concluded, 'Arson cannot be excluded as a cause. If in fact some person or persons were responsible for the deliberate lighting of the fire, then he or they can only be described as irresponsible maniacs, as such resulted in the death of seven people and damage to property well in excess of $100,000.' In fact the bill was $500,000 with the building only partly insured.

An emotional remembrance was held in the gutted hall. More than 150 Salvationists stood in the debris of scattered and burnt music sheets, instruments, charred wood and twisted metal. Major Martin told the congregation the most important item in the hall had been saved. He held aloft the Soldier's Roll, the book that held the name of every Salvationist that had passed through the Adelaide Corps.[69] During the ceremony Mr Simm's beloved taxi remained outside the Palace on an expired meter[70], awaiting its first day of work. It would never make that journey.

This fire was a tragedy waiting to happen. With a locked fire escape, it was a death trap. The door should have contained a panic bar (push bar door). Such doors cannot be locked from the inside, operate in minimal visibility and simply require a light push to open. The People's Palace

Remembrance in the Congress Hall Shell
Salvation Army

was a building which did not need to comply with South Australia's Building Act which came into force in January 1974.

There were other mistakes. The staff was untrained. Doyle relied on residents to ring the fire brigade and delayed his inspection of the accommodation closest to the fire. The biggest failing, however, in both the William Booth and People's Palace fires was the absence of water sprinklers.

Close Up of Remembrance Ceremony in the Congress Hall Shell
Salvation Army

Building Fires and the Case for Sprinklers

How can a catastrophic multi-death fire such as the William Booth be prevented? Recent research has demonstrated a properly designed, installed and maintained water sprinkler system, in conjunction with an integrated fire protection system would preclude such a large loss of life. This life-saving device was invented before Thomas Edison invented the first practical light bulb.

The first practical automatic sprinkler was introduced by Henry Parmelee in 1874 in the United States. Frederick Grinnell further developed Parmalee's design, greatly increasing the sensitivity of the sprinkler system. In 1886, a 'Grinnell' sensitive automatic sprinkler system was installed in the Laycock Son & Nettleton building in South Melbourne. The sprinkler system saved the bed-making factory in the very same year. An Australian historian, H.W. Marryatt, who has written a definitive book on the subject, has waxed lyrical on the 'remarkable and well documented performance' of the Grinnell automatic sprinkler

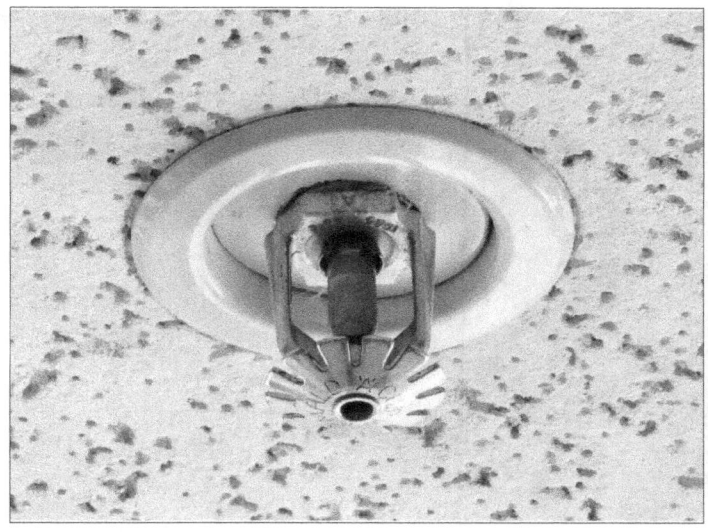

A Typical Sprinkler

during its first 100 years of use in Australia and in discussing the Laycock fire, noted it was in operation soon after Frederick Grinnell had designed and introduced it to the United States.[71]

Sir William Mather, a British fire suppression pioneer had secured the patent rights for the entire world outside the continent of North America. Through Mather, the 'Grinnell sprinkler' quickly spread across the entire globe, from England to the Laycock building in Melbourne.

The capacity of the water sprinkler to save lives was immediately apparent. There have been attempts in the United States to compare death statistics in sprinklered versus non-sprinklered buildings since their introduction. A remarkable early example was in 1913 when the records of the Boston Manufacturers' Mutual Fire Insurance Company (BMMFIC) were examined.[72] In a lecture entitled 'The Automatic Sprinkler as a Life Saver', it was noted there had been only 12 deaths in the factory buildings insured by the company since the introduction of the automatic sprinkler in 1874. Three victims had re-entered a burning building to save personal effects and four firemen had died in their course of duty. The examination concluded that there were 'only five employees who were not able to save themselves in a period of 39 years.' The sprinklers were protecting an estimated 1.5 million factory workers during the period of the study.

1911 Triangle Shirtwaist Factory Fire
Cornell University

One plant not covered by the BMMFIC was the Triangle Shirtwaist factory in New York where 146 perished, mainly young women. As a comparison, the 39 year period (1972 to 2011) shows 21 deaths per 1.5 million workers, or about 75 per cent more than the five the

BMMFIC reported.[73] As the majority of these types of premises remain without sprinklers, the conclusion can be drawn that the sprinkler-protected BMMFIC workers were experiencing a much lower fire death rate than their unprotected modern counterparts.

Another study by the National Fire Protection Association (NFPA) in 1930, entitled 'Loss of Life in Sprinklered Fires', examined 52,303 fires in sprinklered buildings from 1898 to 1930. Only 119 (0.002 per cent) of these fires had a fatality, with the total number of deaths equalling 386, most in explosions.[74] In only 12 cases (10 per cent) was the sprinkler system unsatisfactory, either due to sub-standard installations, inadequate water supplies or objects blocking the spray. The majority of people died 'in serious explosions or rapidly spreading flash fires which sprinklers should not be expected to control.' The report confirmed 'conclusively the value of automatic sprinklers as a safeguard to life against fire. It is apparent that even when the hazard of explosions or flash fires exists they are effective in many cases.'

Even more tellingly, the authors were amazed there were only two cases in the NFPA records where loss of life had occurred in a 'mercantile, hotel, apartment or similar occupancy', where sprinklers were present. As the twentieth century progressed, sprinklers were slowly extending beyond manufacturing structures to other so-called 'places of assembly', such as premises where people get together to work, live (for example, William Booth), be educated and entertained. And it is here that a qualitative comparison can be made. In the period studied in the 1930 survey 1,538 people were killed in six unsprinklered US building fires alone: Iroquois Theatre, (1903, 602 dead); Collinwood School (1908, 175 dead); Rhoads Opera House (1908, dead); Cleveland Clinic (1929, 125 dead) and Ohio Penitentiary (1930, 320 dead).

There are a number of caveats to these two early NFPA studies. In its early days, the NFPA (and they were not unusual in this regard) was rather casual in statistical methods and claims.[75] The reports do not compare like building types, with and without sprinklers, and it is not clear who was surveyed. But even if these studies cannot be regarded as comprehensive, statistically sound surveys, they do provide strong early anecdotal indicators of the association of sprinklers with preservation of life. At minimum they showed there were very few fire deaths in a sample of sprinklered properties, amongst the majority that were not.

More recent analyses show that sprinklers almost eliminate multi-fatality catastrophes such as the William Booth. When fires do occur with large death tolls (see Appendix 2), such as the US Station nightclub fire where 100 perished in 2003, the ensuing fire investigation report inevitably leads with the observation that the absence of sprinklers was critical to the large loss. Both a full-scale replica of the Station nightclub as well as a computer simulation demonstrated a water sprinkler system would have been able to control the fire, even when the walls were swathed in highly flammable foam insulation.[76] The 100 crosses that mark the memorial[77] (where the Station nightclub once stood) would not be there if sprinklers had been installed. This building had been exempted from carrying sprinklers as it was built before the state fire code (in this case, Rhode Island) which required them came into effect. Rhode Island has now strengthened its fire codes but other states have not.

Sprinklers are not only effective in properties with the potential for enormous loss of life, they save lives in all kinds of fires. The NFPA's latest sprinkler report (2013) found that the rate of deaths per thousand fires was 86 per cent lower in all structures combined.[78] When sprinklers are present, they prevent all but the extremely rare one or two person deaths.[79]

Although a negligible occurrence, what are the circumstances that have led to one or (even rarer) two person deaths in sprinklered buildings? Excluding explosions and flash fires, fatal injuries can occur in buildings with properly maintained sprinklers when victims:

(a) act irrationally;

(b) re-enter a building (as cited in the BMMFIC's 1913 study);

(c) are incapacitated;

(d) are firefighting (1913 example);

(e) are close to the origin of the fire; or

(f) are elderly or in poor health (for example, in a nursing home).[80]

The 2013 NFPA report showed most of the sprinklered fatalities are individual deaths with the victims having multiple characteristics from this six point list, such as being near the point of ignition, elderly and incapacitated.

BUILDING FIRES AND THE CASE FOR SPRINKLERS

The remains of the Station Nightclub
West Warwick Fire Department

In Australia, since 1966, there have been 163 fire fatalities in buildings where people assemble[81], the latest in 2011 when 14 residents were killed in the Quakers Hill Nursing Home fire in New South Wales.

The life preserving statistics are transparent, so why are sprinklers not a requirement in all buildings where people get together — in these places of assembly?

There are several myths surrounding this technology. The first is cost. Although not inexpensive (the precise costs of design, installation, inspection and maintenance vary according to building type, including whether the sprinklers are fitted into a new or retrofitted in an existing building), the 2013 NFPA report notes 'sprinkler costs are often over-estimated'[82] by exaggerating inspection and maintenance costs, labour costs, water damage costs and undervaluing long term benefits. Their effectiveness in eliminating large multi-fatality catastrophes (and in preventing almost all fires from developing into fatal fires), in reducing non-fatal injuries and in preserving property means they are cost-effective.

Another myth relates to their reliability. Properly maintained they are exceptional in this regard. In Australia from 1886 to 1986, sprinklers controlled 99.46 per cent of fires that occurred in water-protected premises. 'Over sensitivity' is not an issue — they only activate in real fires and only the sprinkler heads directly above the fire activate, each head acts independently. In the same Australian survey, it was shown that more than 80 per cent of fires were controlled with one or two sprinkler heads only.[83]

The 2013 NFPA report showed that when present in fires large enough to cause activation, US sprinklers operated in 91 per cent of reported structural fires, excluding buildings under construction or with partial installations.[84] Of the 9 per cent of the sprinkler systems that failed, 93 per cent of those failures were due to human error, a failure either in design, selection, maintenance or operation. These mirror the early NFPA studies. If these 'human failings could be eliminated, the overall sprinkler failure rate would drop from the estimated 9 per cent of reported fires to 0.6 per cent.' The resulting 99.4 per cent success rate almost precisely matches Australia's rate of 99.5 per cent as recorded in 1986.

They are a proven life saver, yet tens of thousands have died in theatres, clubs, shops, hostels, backpackers, hotels and nursing homes in Australia, the United States and the rest of the world, with the latest calamity occurring in Brazil in 2013 when 242[85] young lives were lost in the Kiss nightclub. Sprinklers were not present in any of these conflagrations because they were not mandatory, and that is the nub of the problem.

A comparison between the United States and Australia is appropriate as both are a federation of states, each state with a separate fire code. From 2002, a new federal law required all newly constructed nursing homes in Australia to install water sprinklers. Victoria and Queensland applied the law retroactively, requiring all aged home buildings to fit them regardless of construction date. There have been no fatalities in a nursing home in Victoria and Queensland since 2002.[86] As sprinklers in Australia are 99.5 per cent reliable this is logical consequence, even in nursing homes where the elderly residents are particularly vulnerable. The absence of sprinklers contributed to the 16 dead in a Connecticut nursing home and 14 in a Tennessee nursing home (both in 2003).

It is an inescapable conclusion that the 14 deaths in New South Wales in 2011 were a tragedy that could have been avoided. This was confirmed when a single sprinkler head extinguished a fire in a full-scale replica of the Quakers Hill Nursing Home. The level of protection of lives depends on where you are born or choose to live, work and be entertained. All states and territories in Australia should have enforced the retrofitting of all nursing homes in 2002, if not earlier. In addition, it was estimated that the Victorian installations would save $100 million in fire damage bills by 2020.[87] Sprinklers not only save lives, they save money.

The importance of building a structure with fireproof materials, having sufficient exits, staff training, fire inspections and first line firefighting equipment (such as extinguishers) should never be underestimated. Sprinklers do not work in isolation, they must be part of an integrated fire protection system. But, whether accidentally or maliciously started, fires should be anticipated with the most efficient measure available and water sprinklers dramatically reduce the risk of multiple death fires.

The Drums Used to Incinerate the
Whiskey Au Go Go Nightclub
Queensland Police Museum

Yet the same problem has persisted since the introduction of sprinklers in the late nineteenth century: differing and inconsistent applications in their use. Differences between building use types (nightclub, hotels, theatres, nursing homes), differences according to when the building was constructed and differences between states. There are differences in costs between fitting out these building use types and sprinklers do not eliminate the possibility of death altogether. They do, however, reduce the risk to negligible levels and certainly eliminate the large scale calamities that have occurred since buildings have been erected.

The ultimate absurdity is that Grinnell conceived, designed and manufactured his sprinklers within walking distance of the Station nightclub, 122 years before it was incinerated.

Unless there is a policy change, unless sprinklers for all types of assembly and institutional buildings (regardless of age) are uniformly mandated across all states and countries, the events described in this book will continue to occur. The only difference will be the names of the dead and maimed.

Quakers Hill Nursing Home
New South Wales Director of Public Prosecutions

Appendix 1

Fatal Australian Place of Assembly Fires Since 1966

William Booth Memorial Home	1966	**30**
Whiskey Au Go Go	1973	**15**
Savoy Hotel	1975	**15**
People's Palace	1975	**7**
Luna Park Ghost Train	1979	**7**
Rembrandt Apartments	1981	**9**
Pacific Nursing Home	1981	**16**
Downunder Hostel	1989	**6**
Oakdale Guest House	1990	**5**
Palm Grove Hostel	1991	**12**
Kew Cottages	1996	**9**
The Palace Backpackers Hostel	2000	**15**
Sea Breeze Lodge Boarding House	2002	**3**
Quakers Hill Nursing Home	2011	**14**

Appendix 2

US Deadliest Non-Terrorist Fires Per Decade Since 1900*

Iroquois Theatre	1903	**602**
Triangle Shirtwaist Factory	1911	**146**
Cleveland Clinic	1929	**125**
Ohio Penitentiary	1930	**320**
Cocoanut Grove	1942	**492**
Our Lady of the Angels School	1958	**95**
Golden Age Nursing Home	1963	**63**
Beverly Hills Supper Club	1977	**165**
DuPont Plaza	1986	**97**
Happyland	1990	**87**
Station Nightclub	2003	**100**

*Excluding terrorist attacks and explosions. Since 1900 in the United States there has been at least one major multi-fatality building fire every decade and often more. The total of the non-terrorist deadliest fires per decade equals a minimum of 2292 deaths.

References

This is a work of non-fiction. The quoted conversations are taken verbatim from court records, coroners' reports, interviews with the participants and other archival material.

Principal Primary Sources

Unless otherwise referenced the information for this book come from:

Coroner's Report 67/316 — William Booth Memorial Fire, Public Record Office Victoria.

Coroner's Report 137/1975 — Fire at People's Palace Adelaide, State Records of South Australia.

Acknowledgements

A special thanks to those who were there, this is your story:

> **Charles Amey**
>
> **Kelvin Fitness**
>
> **Les Gray**
>
> **Laurie Lavelle**
>
> **Desmond Panizza**
>
> **Jeff Penberthy**
>
> **Trevor Reed**

~

Special thanks are also due to those who gave tireless technical assistance during the development of this narrative and reviewed the manuscript:

Ross Brogan
Lecturer/Subject Co-ordinator Fire Investigation subjects, Charles Sturt University

Dr John D. DeHaan
Director, Fire-Ex Forensics; Author of *Kirk's Fire Investigation*, 7th edition, Prentice Hall, 2011

Dr David J. Icove
UL Professor of Practice, The University of Tennessee; Co-author of *Kirk's Fire Investigation*, 7th edition, Prentice Hall, 2011

Mitch Parish
Former member of the New South Wales Police Arson Squad

ACKNOWLEDGEMENTS

John Hall
National Fire Protection Association (Sprinklers)

Thank you also to the following for giving their expertise on the death of Vincent Fox:

Associate Professor David Ranson
Deputy Director, Victorian Institute of Forensic Medicine; Adjunct Clinical Associate Professor Department of Forensic Medicine, Monash University

Dr Marc Krouse
Chief Deputy Medical Examiner, Tarrant County, Texas.

More thanks to:

Lindsay Cox
Territorial Archivist, The Salvation Army Australia, Southern Territory

Appreciation is also extended to:

Marty Aherns
National Fire Protection Association

Walt Beattie
Beattie Fire Protection & Risk Consulting

Malcolm Bryant
South Australia Metropolitan Fire Service Historian

Barbara Burnheim
For the review and suggesting the main title

Cathy Johnstone
For editing this book

Barbara McCumisky
Metropolitan Fire and Emergency Services Board Education Officer, Melbourne

Jamie Novak
Novak Investigations

Jan Smith
Metropolitan Fire and Emergency Services Board, Melbourne

Kristina Starnawski
Metropolitan Fire and Emergency Services Board Historian, Melbourne

Nancy Schwartz
National Fire Protection Association

Endnotes

1. http://en.wikipedia.org/wiki/Little_Lon_district, quoting Justin McCarthy, *The Commonwealth Block, Melbourne; Archaeological Investigation Report, Volume 1; Historical and Archaeological Report*, Australian Construction Services prepared for The Department of Administrative Services and Telecom Australia, 1989, p. 55.
2. 'Nobodies', *The Age*, 24 August 1966.
3. *William Booth Memorial Home for Men, Little Lonsdale Street, Melbourne, Victoria 1916-1967. A Brief History*, Salvation Army Records.
4. *The War Cry*, 5 February 1915.
5. 'Another Memorial to our Founder', *The Victory*, 1 March 1946.
6. Died 20 August 1912.
7. 'Standing by the Working Man', *The Victory*, 1 May 1922.
8. Ibid.
9. Milligrams per 100 milliliters.
10. 'Not an Institution but a Home', *The War Cry*, 19 April 1947.
11. Ibid.
12. For example, it is not mentioned in *The Australian Book of Disasters* by Larry Writer, Murdoch Books Pty Ltd, 2011.
13. *The Age*, 4/5/6 October 1966.
14. ' Fires of Which the Brigade has Been Notified or Has Attended at the Wm. Booth Hostel in the Last 38 Years', Melbourne Fire Brigade Records.
15. Kelvin Fitness, pers. comm.
16. FOX VINCENT GREGORY: Service Number – NX162210 – 09 Sep 1903: Place of Birth – HOBART TAS: Place of Enlistment – ADELAIDE RIVER NT: Next of Kin – FOX PERCIVAL [Series B883, Control Symbol NX162210, National Archives Canberra, Digitized].
17. Per square inch.
18. Based on the scale map of the third floor (as found in the Coroner's report, page 5), equalling 256 rooms in total. No two sources can agree to the exact number of rooms that were present

on the day of the fire. A Melbourne Fire Brigade report states 278 cubicles.
19 David Eric Ferguson, testimony, Coroner's Report.
20 *The Australian*, 25 August 1966 and Coroner's Report.
21 Victor James Reiger, testimony, Coroner's Report.
22 James Patrick Cannard, testimony, Coroner's Report.
23 Ernest Reid, testimony, Coroner's Report.
24 *Backdraft*, 1991.
25 The soda-acid extinguisher is a container filled with water and a smaller container filled with separate containers of bicarbonate soda and sulphuric acid (which created a pressurised gas that expelled the water).
26 *The Age*, 15 August 1966.
27 *The Australian*, 15 August 1966.
28 Ibid.
29 *The Age*, 15 August 1966.
30 Ibid.
31 Ibid.
32 John William Webster and Gordon Arthur, testimonies, Coroner's Report.
33 J. Patterson, 'Fire and Loss of Life at Salvation Army — William Booth Home Hostel', Melbourne Fire Brigade, 25 August 1966.
34 Timings based on extract from the 'Radio Log Book, re fire at Salvation Army Hostel 462 Little Lonsdale Street Melbourne, Saturday 13 August 1966', Melbourne Fire Brigade.
35 'Fire at William Booth Memorial Home. 462 Little Lonsdale Street Melbourne', Report by T. Reed, 16 August 1966. Numerous interviews with Trevor Reed.
36 'Fire at William Booth Memorial Home', Report by W. J. Barker, Melbourne Fire Brigade.
37 'Fire at the William Booth', Report of E. A. Scown, Melbourne Fire Brigade, 16 August 1966.
38 'Fire at William Booth Memorial Home, 462 Lt. Lonsdale Street Melbourne', Report by R. Treverton, Melbourne Fire Brigade, 16 August 1966.
39 *The Age*, 15 August 1966.

ENDNOTES

40 Treverton, 'Fire at William Booth Memorial Home, 462 Lt. Lonsdale Street Melbourne 16 August 1966', Melbourne Fire Brigade.
41 *The Age*, 15 August 1966.
42 Les Gray, 'Salvation Army William Booth Memorial Hostel Fire' in *Water Off*, Volume 10 No 2, May 2006.
43 Ibid.
44 *The Sun*, 15 August 1966; 'Ghosts of the William Booth', *Time*, 30 October 1989.
45 Gray, 'Salvation Army William Booth Memorial Hostel Fire' in *Water Off*
46 *The Age*, 15 August 1966.
47 Ibid.
48 Pers. comm., Dr Marc Krouse, MD, Chief Deputy Medical Examiner, Tarrant County, Texas. The Medical Examiner, David Hossack, may have been indicating there was both an extradural and subdural haemorrhage, but the most likely interpretation of the testimony is he used the terms interchangeably. A subdural would have impaired Fox's response to the fire.
49 Many thanks to David Ranson, Deputy Director, Victorian Institute of Forensic Medicine for his considerable assistance in interpreting the medical examiner's report.
50 *The War Cry*, 24 September 1966.
51 *Herald,* 16 August 1966.
52 *The Age*, 16 August 1966.
53 *The War Cry*, 3 September 1966.
54 S. Wilde, *Life Under The Bells: A History Of The Metropolitan Fire Brigade, Melbourne 1891–1991*, Longman Chesire, Melbourne.
55 *The Age*, 15 August 1966.
56 In the 1990s.
57 *The News*, 22 April 1975.
58 Brett Allen, testimony, Coroner's Report. *The News*, 22 April 1975.
59 Henry Edward Day, testimony, Coroner's Report.
60 Harold Ray Doyle, testimony, Coroner's Report.
61 *The News*, 22 April 1975.
62 *The News*, 22 April 1975.
63 Ibid.

64   Newspapers at the time reported the brigade were there within five minutes of the alarm being raised. This is contrary to the testimony at the Coroner's inquest. Doyle stated he detected smoke 'about 3.10 or 3.15 am'.

65   Charles Amey, pers. comm. and Desmond John Panizza, testimony, Coroner's Report.

66   *The News*, 22 April 1975.

67   Desmond John Panizza, testimony, Coroner's Report & pers. comm.

68   22 April 1975. Unidentified newspaper.

69   *The Advertiser*, 5 May 1975.

70   *The News*, 22 April 1975.

71   H.W. Marryatt, *Fire: A Century Of Automatic Sprinkler Protection In Australia And New Zealand 1886–1986*, North Melbourne, Victoria, 1988. Australian Fire Protection Association in co-operation with National Fire Protection Association and National Fire Sprinklers Association Inc USA.

72   *Quarterly of the National Fire Protection Association*, July 1913.

73   'In recent years there have been about 5 fire deaths per year in structure fires in manufacturing or processing properties, and there have been about 14 million people employed in manufacturing. If you multiply the 5 deaths per year by 39 years, you get 195 deaths and if you pro-rate that to 1.5 million workers, it translates into 21 deaths per 39 years and 1.5 million workers, or about 75% more than the early 20th century insurer reported. Add to that the fact that fire death rates generally have been trending sharply down over the past century and the fact that most factory fires still do not benefit from sprinklers, and you have a basis for saying that those 1.5 million workers were probably experiencing a much lower fire death rate than their early 20th century (and late 19th century) counterparts in unsprinklered factories.' Statistics and wording provided by John Hall, National Fire Protection Association.

74   66 per cent (explosions). Of these 119 cases where a death occurred, 65 (55.4 per cent) were effective in extinguishing the fire or holding it in check. Explosions before or in the early stage of the fire crippled the sprinkler system in 24 (20.5 per cent) instances. In ten cases the sprinkler system was shut off.

ENDNOTES

75   John Hall, National Fire Protection Association, pers. comm.

76   William Lytle Grosshandler, Nelson P Bryner, Daniel Madrzykowski, Kenneth Kuntz, 'Report of the technical investigation of The Station nightclub fire', United States Federal Emergency Management Agency; Building and Fire Research Laboratory (U.S.); Fire Research Division; National Construction Safety Team Act (U.S.).

77   Soon to be permanent.

78   Table 4.1 from John R. Hall, Jr., *U.S. Experience with Sprinklers*, NFPA Fire Analysis and Research Division, June 2013, using 2007–2011 data.

79   Current knowledge indicates that, with one exception (see below) there have been only very rare occurrences where one or two persons have died in a sprinklered buildings. The victims are usually highly susceptible to the effects of a fire, being elderly or less mobile for example. The National Fire Protection Association concludes (pers. comm.) that, as there is no census of every fire that has occurred in US sprinklered buildings since 1874, it is not impossible, but unlikely, that many if any, fires with three or more deaths would go unrecorded.

The one exception occurred in New York, March 2009, where four died. The building was a single storey board and care occupancy of wood-frame construction. At the time of the fire, there were nine residents and two staff members present. A building fire alarm system was installed consisting of smoke detectors in sleeping areas and most common spaces. Heat detectors were installed in the kitchen, laundry room and shower room as well as in the attic space. A wet-pipe sprinkler system was also provided. Two sprinkler heads operated as designed, though they were not effective as the fire started outside the structure and spread inside. The fire originated in a plastic rubbish container on an attached porch. The fire spread into the attic and then throughout the rest of the building. The cause was not determined but investigators reported that human activity was involved in some way. Stephen G. Badger, *Catastrophic Multiple-Death Fires for 2009*, National Fire Protection Association Fire Analysis and Research Division, September 2010.

80   John R. Hall, Jr., US Experience With Sprinklers.
81   Refer to Appendix 1. 35 deaths in 11 separate boarding house and hotel fires were identified before 1966 in an undated study by Paratek, 'Budget Accommodation Australia - Fire Safety - We Have a Right to Survive', (web).
82   John R. Hall, Jr., US Experience With Sprinklers
83   H.W. Marryatt, *Fire: A Century Of Automatic Sprinkler Protection In Australia And New Zealand 1886–1986*.
84   John R. Hall, Jr., US Experience With Sprinklers.
85   At time of publication. Many are still in critical conditions.
86   *The Courier Mail*, 27 November 2011 (web). See also *The Sydney Morning Herald*, 19 November 2011 (web).
87   *The Courier Mail*, 27 November 2011 (web).

Photographs and Maps

vi   The William Booth Memorial Home After The Fire.
vii   The People's Palace, Adelaide.
viii   Casualties in the Central Hallway of the William Booth Memorial Home. Two Police 'Roundsmen', Reporters based in the Press-Room next to the Russell Street Police Headquarters, are visible in the rear. Ken Hickey (Glasses) and Noel Harley (Notepad).
xi   Salvation Army Red Shield.
xvi   William Booth.
xviii   Western Wall of the William Booth Post Fire.
xx   Tipperary Rear Escape Stairs, The People's Palace.
xxi   Faulty Fireproof Door on the William Booth 3rd Floor.
xxii   Salvation Army Crest and the Reference to the 'Fire' of the Holy Spirit.
2   Kelvin Fitness and Wife.
4   Wet Riser in the Fire Fighting Recess Next to Fox's Room.
5   3rd Floor Layout.
8   Booking Clerk Ernest Reid in his Cubicle.
9   The Heater that caused the Fire and a Table showing the Effects of a Backdraft and Flashover.
10   Charred Area of the Floor where the Upturned Heater Burnt.
12   Fuse Box Next to Room 39.
13   The Construction of Fox's Room Enclosed with a Masonite Ceiling.
14   Plan Showing the Construction of Fox' Room.
15   The Fire Hose Lies where it was Dropped.
16   Fox's Room was Obliterated.
17   The Fire in Full Flight.
18   4th Floor Hallway Showing the Effects of the Superheated Upper Layer.
20   A Flashover.
21   The Escape Stairs Showing Scattered Clothing Items.
23   The Rooms Next to Fox's Fell like a Pack of Cards.

24   Most Men Were Caged with Cyclone Mesh Covering their Rooms.
26   Close Up of Floor in Fox's Room.
27   Eastern Hills Metropolitan Fire Brigade Headquarters.
28   Gordon Geddes and Wife.
29   Trevor Reed.
29   Alby Hall.
30   Ernie Scown.
31   A Leyland Metz Ladder attended the Conflagration.
33   Les Gray Resuscitating a Victim using the Silvester Method. Station Officer Jack Barker is Directly Behind Gray.
34   A Victim Being Carried by the Fore and Aft Method.
35   A Fireman Being Relieved by an Ambulance Officer.
36   Frantic revival Attempts in the Hallway. Makeshift mortuaries were Established in the Adjoing Dining and Lounge Rooms.
37   The Dire Conditions the Policemen Rescuers Faced in the Showers.
39   Chief Officer Jack Paterson.
40   Carnage in the Shower.
40   A Death Soot Shadow in the Shower.
41   More Death Soot Shadows.
41   A Victim.
42   Firemen Propping Up the Victims Outside.
43   The Devastating Effects of a Flashover and Backdraft on the Body of Fox.
45   Ambulance Officers in front of the Leyland Metz Rescue Ladder.
45   Scenes of Despair Outside the William Booth.
47   Funeral March.
47   Funeral Procession.
48   The Nobodies are Laid to Rest.
49   Order of Services.
53   The People's Palace
54   Sketch Map of the Congress Hall.
56   Foyer of the Congress Hall.
56   Entrance to the Congress Hall from the Administration Area. Likely Access Point for an Arsonist.
57   Aerial View of the Gutted Congress Hall.
58   Gutted Congress Hall.

PHOTOGRAPHS AND MAPS

60   Floor of the Fallen Tipperary Section.
60   Close Up of Furniture Items from the Tipperary Rooms.
61   Sketch Diagram of Bodies Under the Tipperary Exit Which was Locked.
63   Remembrance in the Congress Hall Shell.
64   Close Up of Remembrance Ceremony in the Congress Hall Shell.
65   A Typical Sprinkler.
66   Triangle Shirtwaist Factory Fire.
69   The remains of the Station Nightclub.
71   The Drums Used to Incinerate the Whiskey Au Go Go Nightclub.
72   The Quakers Hill Nursing Home.

Index

Accelerant, 61
Alcohol, xvii, xix, 44
Allen, Brett, 51-52, 55, 57, 62
Ambulance Service, 35
Amey, Charles, 59
Anderson, Les, 25
Andrews, Mr, 15
Arson, xxi, 62
Arthur, Constable, 25, 37

Backdraft, 12-13, 16
Baguley, Leonard, xiv
Barker, Jack (W J), 28-30, 33p
Barry, Brigadier, 46
Belton, Robert, xv
Berry, Stephen, xiii
Berryman, Mr, 57
Beverly Hills Supper Club, 74
Biske, William, xiv
Black, Farnsworth, xiv
Blackwood, James, xiv
Bolt, Henry, 50
Booth, William, xvip, xviii
Boston Manufacturer's Mutual Fire Insurance Company, 66-67, 68
Brown, Robert, 25
Buckle, John, 1
Burns, Keith, xv

Cannard, James, 11-12, 15-16, 22
Carbon monoxide, 25, 43-44
Cleveland Clinic, 67, 74
Cocoanut Grove, 74
Collingwood School, 67
Conway, Francis, xiv

INDEX

Connecticut Nursing Home, 70
Cooper, David, xiv
Coroner, x, 19, 50

Darlow, R., x
Dawson, Harry, xiv
Day, Mr, 52
Dean, James, xiv
Deacon, Reg, 32
Dillon, Constable, 26
Downunder Hostel, 73
Doyle, Harold, 52, 54-55, 64
Dupont Plaza, 70

Edison, Thomas, 65
Extradural haemorrhage, 43

Farr, James, xiv, xix
Ferguson, David, 6
Firemen, 27-44, 58-59
Fitness, Kelvin, 2, 15, 21
Flashover, 19, 20p, 43
Fort, Douglas, xv
Fox, Vincent, xiv, 3-4, 6-10, 22, 42-44

Geddes, Gordon, 28-30, 35-36
Gill Memorial Home, 42
Golden Age Nursing Home, 74
Governor Hotel, 59
Gray, Les, 32, 33p, 48
Grinnell, Frederick, 65-66, 72

Haas, Frederick, xiv, 44
Hall, Alby, 29-30
Happyland, 74
Hartley, David, xiv, 24-25
Haywood, Kenny, 22-25
Heater, 7-8, 9p, 10p

Hooson, Edward, xiv
Hovath, Mrs, 57
Hydrant, 3-4, 29

Insley, William, 25, 38-39
Iroquois Theatre, 67, 74

Jones, Steven, xv

Kew Cottages, 73
Kiss Nightclub, 70

Lamaur, Edward, xiv
Lamour, Edward, xiv
Lavelle, Laurie, 37-38
Laycock Building, 65-66
Lennard, Benny, 23-24
Leyland Metz Ladder, 31p, 45p
Lloyd, John, xiv
Luna Park Ghost Train, 73

Mackenzie, Ronald, xiv
Mangan, Joseph, xiv
Marchant, William, xiv
Marryatt, H, 65
Martin, Major, 63
Mather, William, 66
McKenzie, John, xiv
McNeice, Herbert, xiv
Metropolitan Hotel, 6, 23
Miller, James, xv
Millcock, *see* Hydrant

National Fire Protection Association, 67-70
Nunn, Ivan, 32, 37

Oakdale Guest House, 73
Ohio Penitentiary, 67, 74

INDEX

Our Lady of the Angels School, 74

Pacific Nursing Home, 73
Palm Grove Hostel, 73
Panizza, Desmond, 59, 62
Parmalee, Henry, 65
Pascoe, H, x
Paterson, Jack, 28, 33p, 38, 42, 44, 46
Penberthy, Jeff, 32, 35
People's Palace, viip, xx, 51-64, 73
Places of Assembly, 67, 69
Policemen, 25-26, 58
Prince Henry's Hospital, 42
Proto Breathing Apparatus, 38
Pyrolysis, 10

Quakers Hill Nursing Home, 69, 72p, 73
Quinlan, Garnet, xv

Radiator *see* Heater
Rainsbury, Ken, 32
Rebreather *see* Proto Breathing Apparatus
Reed, Trevor, 29-30, 38, 44, 46
Reid, Ernest, 8p, 11-12, 16, 19-20, 31
Reiger, Major, 3, 7-8, 13-14, 16, 19-20, 35
Rembrandt Hotel, 73
Rhoads Opera House, 67
Roberts, David, xv
Robertson, David, 21-22
Robertson, George, xv
Royal Melbourne Hospital, 42

Savoy Hotel, 73
Scown, Ernie, 29-30, 37
Sea Breeze Lodge Boarding House, 73
Showler, Andrew, xv
Silvester Manual Resuscitation, 32, 33p
Simm, William, xv, 52

Sleeman, Lionel, 32
Sprinklers, 48, 50, 65-72
St Vincent's Hospital, 42, 44
Station Nightclub, 68, 69p, 72, 74
Statton, Charles, xv
Subdural haemorrhage, 43

Tennessee Nursing Home, 70
The Palace Backpackers Hostel, 73
Tipperary Accommodation, xx, 51, 55, 59
Treverton, Roy, 31-32, 38, 46
Triangle Shirtwaist Factory Fire, 66, 74
Tueno, Frank, 44
Turner, James, xv

Udale, Frank, xv

Vickerman, James, xv
Vigor, Arthur, xv

Wade, Peter, 29-30, 37
Webster, John, 25-26, 37
Wet Riser, 3
Whelan, Gordon, xv
Whiskey Au Go Go, xix, 71p, 73
William Booth Memorial Home, vip, viiip, xvi-xix, 1-50, 68, 73
Wilson, Thomas, xv
Wiseman, General, 62
Workman's Metropole, xvii
Wright, James, xv

YMCA, 59

www.ingramcontent.com/pod-product-compliance
Lightning Source LLC
Chambersburg PA
CBHW060516300426
44112CB00017B/2693